If Jesus Chri[st] _____
tians believe, _____
issue for huma[n] _____ [cl]ear
him, and to rec[eive him as Lord and Saviour. This book c[learl]y sets out the claims and
the commendation of the eternal Son of God, the
Saviour of the world.
The Bishop of Chester,
The Rt. Revd. Michael A. Baughen

'Clear, contemporary, direct and above all thoroughly biblical.'
Peter Lewis,
Cornerstone Evangelical Church, Nottingham

Here are lively explanations of ten stories from John's Gospel describing how 'meeting with Jesus' affected different people (often very like ourselves) in different ways. Melvin Tinker, unlike many of us clergymen, is never dull! I hope all who read these stories will enjoy them as I have done, and that some, for the first time, will have their eyes opened as to what 'meeting with Jesus' can mean for them, here and now.
Dick Lucas,
St Helen's Bishopgate, London.

Melvin Tinker believes the Bible to be true and therefore relevant. His ten encounters with Jesus are a careful explanation of what actually happened when various 'ordinary people' (like us) met this enigmatic and remarkable man. But they are written in a refreshing and accessible style and are always related to contemporary life so that the incidents are brought into the present with a compelling insistence.

Ranald Macaulay,
L'Abri Fellowship

'Honest, down-to-earth teaching for honest, down-to-earth people.'
J I Packer,
Regent College, Vancouver.

CLOSE ENCOUNTERS

*Meeting with Jesus
and the Difference it Makes*

Melvin Tinker

Christian Focus Publications

This book is gratefully dedicated to Percy and Lois Johnson whose life and words commended Jesus Christ to the author.

© 1996 Melvin Tinker
ISBN 1-85792-132-1

Cover design by Donna Macleod
Scripture quotations are from the Holy Bible,
New International Version, © 1973, 1978, 1984 by
International Bible Society

Published by
Christian Focus Publications Ltd.
Geanies House, Fearn, Ross-shire,
IV20 1TW, Scotland, Great Britain.

Printed and bound in Great Britain by
Cox & Wyman Ltd, Reading, Berkshire.

Contents

Introduction

Saul of Tarsus, Augustine of Hippo, John Wesley, Elizabeth Fry, C.S. Lewis, Cliff Richard, Helen Shapiro, Chris Akabussi. What do they all have in common (other than the fact that they are famous)? It is that they all claim that in some way they have met with Jesus Christ. They are not alone. For nearly 2,000 years, countless millions of people from differing backgrounds and cultures have made similar claims. Although the details may vary, the substance of the claims remains the same: Jesus of Nazareth, a well attested historical figure, is alive, is to be worshipped as God and has the power to change lives.

That is some claim!

The purpose of this book is to help back up that claim by looking at eleven episodes recorded in John's account of the life of Jesus, in which several quite different people had encounters with him which were to radically transform their lives. Admittedly, there has been some selectivity of the events recorded by John (which writer isn't selective?), but like the cumulative effect of a series of clues in a great detective story, they all add up to the one inescapable conclusion – Jesus is no ordinary person. On the contrary, he is someone who makes extraordinary claims, exhibiting extraordinary power, and can be known today.

The events recorded by John speak for themselves. However, in order to allow the emotive force of what Jesus says to take its full effect, on occasions the words have been paraphrased and the practical implications specifically drawn out. This is simply part of the expository preaching style of the book. But since J I Packer once remarked 'The Bible is God preaching', hopefully such rewording will be in line with God's own chosen method of self-disclosure.

Has God revealed himself? Read on and draw your own conclusions.

1

Jesus meets a doubter
(John 20:24-31)

Let me give ten reasons why I don't wash:

1. I was made to wash as a child and that put me off.
2. People who wash are hypocrites, everyone knows that, for they reckon they are cleaner than other people.
3. There are so many different kinds of soap, I couldn't possibly decide how to choose between them.
4. I used to wash, but it got rather boring so I gave it up.
5. I only wash on special occasions, like Easter and Christmas.
6. I'm still young. When I get older and a little dirtier I might turn to washing then.
7. I really don't have time, I am far too busy to wash.
8. None of my other friends wash, so why should I?
9. The bathroom's never warm enough.

10. People who make soap are only after your money.

You will have noticed that this list is remarkably similar to the standard objections to Christianity and church attendance, which, when put like that, highlight how unreasonable they are. But what about this for an objection?: 'What I can't stand about Christians is that they are so gullible. It's all a matter of faith. As for me, I'm a down-to-earth sort of person, hard nosed. I deal with facts not faith – give me some proof.' Is the objector right? Is faith somehow opposed to facts and therefore more like fantasy, believing six impossible things before breakfast?

The story we are looking at in this chapter demonstrates once and for all that it is not a matter of having to choose between faith and facts, but that true faith is based upon facts. This is brought out in this amazing story of the encounter between the disciple Thomas and the risen Lord Jesus in John 20.

That I can't believe
Now Thomas (called Didymus), one of the Twelve, was not with the disciples when Jesus came ... the other disciples told him that they had seen the Lord (20:24-25).

This was the setting: Jesus had been brutally

executed. Consequently the disciples were huddled behind locked doors, hiding in fear lest the Roman authorities do to them what they did to their Master. Suddenly, Jesus appeared out of nowhere. There he was in flesh and blood standing before them. Admittedly it was a transformed body, but a corporeal body nonetheless.

So you can imagine the enthusiasm with which the disciples would have told Thomas the wonderful news that Jesus was the Messiah after all, that death could not hold him.

But how did Thomas reply? 'Marvellous news, just what I've been waiting to hear'? On the contrary: *'Unless I see the nail marks in his hands and put my finger where the nails were, and put my hand into his side, I will not believe it'* (20:25).

That's a stringent demand that Thomas is making, one which would have made any logical positivist proud: 'I don't only want to see him, I want to touch him. And not only do I want to touch him, I want irrefutable proof that he really is the one I saw crucified and not some impostor, and that means feeling the holes in his hands, and inserting my hand into his side which was lacerated by a spear. If I can't do that I won't believe.' Not I can't believe, but I *won't* believe.

Is there not a note of defiance here? Is not Thomas laying down demands which are plainly unreasonable? It certainly seems that way. It is all

very much in line with what Jesus constantly encountered throughout his ministry and which Paul
targets in 1 Corinthians 1, namely, that the 'Jews
demand signs'. In fact, this became a barrier to
belief.

The same principle operates today. We say: I
will devote myself to God *if* he heals my child. I
will follow Jesus *if* he mends my marriage. I will
happily become a Christian *if* God proves himself to me in a tangible way, performing a miracle
on demand. In each of these cases, it is not God
who is called to assess us, but we who are assessing him, demanding that he jump through the
hoops we set up.

In effect we are laying down the conditions God
must meet if he is to have the privilege of our
company. But not only is this the height of arrogance, it is the height of folly. For what if Christianity is true and God refuses (as is his right) to
meet our preconditions? Then we forfeit knowing
him for ever. What if God has given us plenty of
reasons for belief, evidences for trusting him
(which, as we shall see in a moment, he has), and
yet by sticking to our prior demands we ignore
them? Then we are as foolish as the man who loses
his wife because he has laid down that unless she
cooks him perfect eggs for breakfast each morning she can't really love him. The wrong criteria
have been employed.

Seeing is believing?

Whether Thomas was really expecting his demands to be met we can't be sure, but one thing is for certain, he was in for a very big surprise: *A week later his disciples were in the house again, and Thomas was with them. Though the doors were locked, Jesus came and stood among them and said, 'Peace be with you.' Then he said to Thomas, 'Put your finger here; see my hands. Reach out your hand and put it into my side. Stop doubting and believe'* (20:26-27).

How incredibly kind of Jesus! He could have let Thomas stew in his own unbelieving juice. Instead, in a remarkable act of loving condescension, the risen Jesus appears with the specific intention of addressing Thomas. Wonderfully, the first words Jesus utters are words of comfort: 'Peace be with you.'

This is not some pious greeting akin to a sanctimonious 'Bless you', nor the first-century equivalent to our 'Have a nice day'. Here we have the crucified and risen Lord of all creation giving words of deep reassurance, the assurance that there is now peace with God. Through his work on the cross, dying as a sacrifice for sins in the place of rebels like us, he has now cleared the way back to God whereby we can approach him as children of a heavenly Father. Given what Thomas had just done, not only in deserting Jesus with the rest of the disciples, but in exercising sinful unbelief, those were precisely the words he needed to hear most of all.

But in addition to words of reassurance, Jesus issued words of rebuke. 'Alright Thomas, have it your way if you must. Put your finger in my side which was torn for you, touch the nail-scarred hands that were pierced for you. Stop disbelieving and show yourself a believer.' That is the way the original can be translated: 'cease disbelieving and believe'.

Some have taken these verses as a justification for the church to allow doubters into the ranks of its leaders. Thomas doubted, he was a leader, yet he was accepted by Jesus. Thus, they say, we are obliged to do the same; doubting bishops are legitimate. But clearly that was not Jesus' intention. This stands as a ticking off for Thomas, not a commendation of how God loves the critical doubter!

Thomas was being told to stop acting like an unbeliever and instead show himself as a true believer. It is not enough simply to believe in God. Thomas did that, he was a good Jew. It is not enough to be associated with Jesus. Thomas had been with Jesus through thick and thin for nearly three years. Nor is it enough to be with those who follow Jesus. Thomas was at least gathered with the other disciples. Something more is required, and just what that something is can be seen in those immortal words that Thomas uttered, '*My Lord and my God*' (20:28).

Thomas was not being profane at this point. This was not the unthinking reaction of a startled man. This is nothing less than a deep personal profession of faith which must be made by anyone who wishes to become a true Christian. This is not blind faith, for the evidence is now too overwhelming, so much so that Thomas did not even bother with his original demands of touching Jesus. Nor is it some vague belief in the divine Other. Rather, this is believing faith which has Jesus as its object. There are two things about this faith which we need to take to heart.

First, this belief is *confessional*. It involves believing a truth. Who is Jesus? He is Lord and God, that's who. This is an amazing confession when you consider the context. The claim is being made that embodied in this crucified carpenter is none other than the Creator of the universe – he is God. Standing before Thomas in magisterial power is the one who demands our submission to his rule for *de facto* he is the ruler of the world, he is Lord.

But this was not mere head knowledge for Thomas, the equivalent to the Apostles Creed which can so easily roll off the tongue, parrot fashion, without engaging the heart or mind. It is a *personal profession of faith*, hence the possessive pronoun, '*My* Lord and *my* God'.

In other words, what lies at the heart of the Christian faith is not religion as such, but a relationship. There are plenty of people in churches up and down the country who are steeped in religion, going through the motions of church attendance, but who have not the faintest idea of what it means to have a personal relationship with God, simply because they have never come to that point where they have submitted to Jesus as *their* ruler and redeemer.

In the middle of the last century, there was a Vicar in Cornwall by the name of William Haslam.[1] One day, much to his surprise, his gardener became a Christian and he didn't quite know what to make of this. He visited a friend who told him bluntly that the reason why he didn't understand was because he himself was not yet converted.

His friend asked him: 'Have you peace with God?'

To which Haslam replied, 'Of course, God is my friend.'

Pursuing the point further, his colleague asked him, 'How did you get that peace?'

'Oh,' replied the Vicar, 'I get it at the daily service. I get it through prayer and reading and espe-

1. Revd W. Haslam, *From Death Unto Life*, Good News Crusade, St Austell, Cornwall, 1979

cially at Holy Communion. I have made it a rule to carry my sins there every Sunday, and often come away from the holy Sacrament feeling happy and as free as a bird.'

'And how long does this peace last?' enquired his friend.

'I suppose not a week,' said Haslam thoughtfully, 'for I have to do the same thing every Sunday.'

The friend then went on to tell him about the living waters that Jesus promised, welling up from within to eternal life. William Haslam then admitted that he did not know of such a thing, but would dearly love to have it. Then he left.

The following Sunday, Haslam climbed into his pulpit and announced the text, 'What think ye of Christ?' This is how he describes what happened next.

'As I went on to explain the passage, I saw that the Pharisees and Scribes did not know that Christ was the Son of God or that he came to save them. Something was telling me all the time, "You are no better than the Pharisees yourself, you do not believe he is the Son of God and that he came to save you any more than they did."

'I do not remember all I said, but I felt a wonderful light and joy coming into my soul, and I was beginning to see what the Pharisees did not. Whether it was my words or my manner or my look, I know not; but all of a sudden a local preacher, who happened to be in the congregation, stood up and putting up his arms shouted out in a Cornish manner, "The parson is converted! the parson is converted! Hallelujah." And in another moment his voice was lost in the shouts and praises of three or four hundred in the congregation. Instead of rebuking this extraordinary brawling as I would have done at one time, I joined in the outburst of praise.'

He then describes how at least twenty people in the congregation cried out for mercy and professed to find joy and peace in believing, including three members of Haslam's own family. The news spread like wildfire throughout the town that the Vicar had been converted by his own sermon!

Like Haslam and Thomas, it is only too possible to be an acquaintance of Christ and yet not a full-blooded believer in Christ. Many a person has a religious standing and yet knows nothing of the forgiveness and peace Christ alone can bring.

The question raised by this incident is: Have you, like Thomas, come to the point where you have personally come before Christ in heartfelt sorrow and trust saying, 'My Lord and my God'? If not, then whatever you may wish to call yourself, you are not yet a Christian.

Believing is seeing

But you may object saying, 'It was alright for Thomas, he saw Jesus face to face. I would believe if confronted with irrefutable proof like that.' Really? Jesus views the matter differently. *Then Jesus told him, 'Because you have seen me, you have believed, blessed are those who have not seen and yet have believed'* (20:29).

I do not have to travel in a space shuttle and look down upon the world to believe that it is round. Others have done that and I have sufficient reason to trust their testimony. Neither do I have to see Jesus bodily to believe that he has been raised from the dead. Others have seen him and I trust their reports with good cause.[2] All the evidence we need to convince any fair-minded person beyond any reasonable doubt that Jesus is God who became man is to be found in the Bible.

Today, claims are being made in some quarters that we need signs and wonders, special miracles to be performed as part of our evangelism, in order to convince a sceptical generation about the truth of Christianity. John would place a serious question mark against such claims.

As far as he is concerned all the signs and wonders we need are contained in his Gospel. He

2. For example, see George E. Ladd, *I Believe in the Resurrection*, Hodder and Stoughton, 1975.

doesn't say, 'By the way, after reading this you may want some confirmatory proof, so why don't you search out your nearest Christian gathering and ask them to perform a few miracles for you.' Far from it. He writes: *These are written* (including reliable accounts of miracles performed by Jesus) *that you may believe that Jesus is the Christ, and that by believing you may have life in his name* (20:31), that is, genuine spiritual life.

If you think that this is not enough, all I can say is that you are claiming that God and John are mistaken, for they think what has been given is sufficient. Admittedly, the evidence is not exhaustive (John says so himself in verse 25 of the next chapter: *Jesus did many other things as well. If every one of them were written down, I suppose that even the whole world would not have room for the books that would be written*). However, the evidence is substantial and sufficient.

God never asks us to exercise blind faith in becoming a follower of Christ, but he does call us to have an open faith, a reasonable trust in his dear Son, based upon the evidence he has so kindly given in his respect for our integrity. Is such a trust too much to ask for? 'Stop unbelieving and show yourself a believer,' says Jesus to Thomas, and to us.

2

Jesus meets a theology professor
(John 3:1-21)

Life is full of misunderstandings. There is the story of the man who went to the tradesman's entrance of a big house and asked if there were any odd jobs he could do. After a moment's thought the owner said that he would pay him £25 to paint the porch at the front of the house. After only a couple of hours the man came back with the pot of white paint and, pleased as Punch, declared that he'd finished. 'That was very quick,' said the owner. 'No problem, boss,' he replied, 'it wasn't all that big a job. And by the way, it's a Mercedes not a Porsche!'

That is a classic example of the way a misunderstanding can lead to disastrous results.

There is an account in John's Gospel of a man who met with Jesus, who also had some serious misunderstandings of his own; misunderstandings about what it meant to be a 'Christian' and what it was to know God and the eternal life he gives. The man's name was Nicodemus and we read about him in John chapter 3.

21

A night to remember

Now there was a man of the Pharisees named Ni-
codemus, a member of the Jewish ruling council.
He came to Jesus at night and said, 'Rabbi, we
know you are a teacher who has come from God.
For no-one could perform the miraculous signs
you are doing if God were not with him' (3:1-2).

Right at the outset it is vitally important that
we get it clear in our minds just who Nicodemus
was. To begin with, he was very religious. He was
a Pharisee, a Bible man, someone who exhibited
a zeal and love for God that was second to none.

What is more, he was a member of the Jewish
ruling council, indeed, in verse 10 the original has
the definite article, with Jesus referring to Nicodemus as *'the* teacher of Israel'. In other words,
he was the top man, the chief mufti, the equivalent to the Archbishop of Canterbury no less. Aca-
demically he was in a league of his own, very
much like a professor of theology.

But it was not all head knowledge for Nicodemus. Pietistically he was wholly devoted to the
God of his fathers. We might think someone like
that would be more than acceptable to Jesus. Indeed, he seems to be ideal discipleship material.
However, as the story unfolds we discover that
nothing could be further from the truth.

We are told that Nicodemus came by night to
speak to Jesus. That doesn't necessarily mean, as

some commentators have suggested, that he was ashamed to be seen speaking to Jesus during the day, for Nicodemus does not strike one as a timid person. Later in John's Gospel we read that he, along with Joseph of Arimathaea, went to the authorities to request the body of Jesus, which was quite a brave thing to do considering what had just happened (19:38-42).

The point of this little detail of his coming at night is its symbolic significance, namely, that as far as Nicodemus's *spiritual* understanding was concerned, he was living in darkness. For all his theology, his ritual and his 'church upbringing' he was as far away from knowing God's salvation as any man could be. And this is borne out by the rather superior and patronizing stance he takes with Jesus: 'Rabbi, we see that you are a teacher come from God, after all no-one could perform the sort of miracles you do unless God were with him in a special way.' Obviously Nicodemus had come to judge and assess Jesus.

However, in a quick turn of the tables, Jesus' reply must have hit him in the face like a wet towel: 'Oh, you think you see do you? Well, you can see nothing, for no-one can see the kingdom of God unless he is born again.' Let the force of that statement sink in. Jesus is saying to this religious, churchgoing, Bible teacher, the Archbishop himself, that as far as even *seeing*, that is, understanding,

the kingdom of God is concerned, he is totally
blind. What is more he will remain like that unless he is born again.

This is a truth that is not reserved for Nicodemus alone, or people like him, it applies to every
single one of us. Unless a man or woman is born
again, he or she is not even on the starting block
of becoming a true believer. And that, we can be
quite sure, would have taken the wind out of
Nicodemus' sails.

So how does he respond? With a bit of scorn,
as intellectuals can so easily do. He comes out
with a classic 'put down': *'How can a man be
born when he is old?' Nicodemus asked. 'Surely
he cannot enter a second time into his mother's
womb to be born!'* (3:4). 'Good one there, Jesus,
old chap; what is this you're talking about? Some
sort of biological regeneration?' He was trying to
make Jesus look stupid.

A vital truth, not a well-worn cliché
Not being deterred, Jesus twists the knife further:
*'I tell you the truth, unless a man is born of water
and the Spirit, he cannot enter the kingdom of
God. Flesh gives birth to flesh but the Spirit gives
birth to spirit'* (3:5). What does Jesus mean?

Today we hear a lot about 'born-again Christians' as if they are a special subspecies of the
genus 'Christian'; so you have Baptist Christians,

'Steady-on-I-want-to-take-my-time-Christians' and born-again Christians.

When I was a minister near Leeds, I was invited to take part in a local radio live phone-in programme on the James Wale show, a controversial broadcaster who usually had very little time for Christians. The subject I was asked to deal with was the ethical implications of genetic engineering – test-tube babies and the like.

The very first thing he said when we went on the air was: 'Tonight we have Melvin Tinker who is an Anglican vicar. Now tell me, Melvin, what do you think about these "Born-again Christians"?' (What that had to do with genetic engineering still remains a mystery to me!) Unabashed, I admitted that I was one. 'But you can't be,' he replied, 'you are in the Church of England!' I then pointed out gently that all true Christians are born-again Christians, there is no other way one can become a Christian; Jesus said so.

So what does it mean to be born again? And how does it happen?

Quite simply, it is a spiritual transformation on the inside which involves the intervention of the Spirit of God himself. It is something which is nothing short of miraculous. No-one can make himself into a Christian. It is something which God alone accomplishes. That is what is behind the statement in verse 5 that *unless a man is born*

*of water and the Spirit he cannot enter the king-
dom of God.*

This has nothing to do with baptism – infant
or adult. Baptism doesn't make you a Christian
no matter how much water you use. Nor is Jesus
talking about the water of the amniotic fluid in
birth, as if Jesus is saying that as well as being
born naturally of a woman you have to be born
supernaturally of God.

In all probability, what Jesus has in mind here
is a passage from the Old Testament, Ezekiel
36:25-27, which prophesies of a time when God's
people will be washed by water and indwelt by
God's Spirit. 'I will sprinkle clean water on you,
and you will be clean; I will cleanse you from all
your impurities and from all your idols. I will give
you a new heart and put a new spirit in you.'

In other words, this talk of water is metaphori-
cal, used to describe the need for inner cleansing
of our sin which gives rise to a new nature. Water
and spirit, therefore, are not two separate entities,
rather both refer to the same process – the cleansing, renewing work of God's Spirit in our hearts.
'Flesh gives birth to flesh', that is, like begets like,
so spiritual life in man is begotten of the Spirit of
God.

Therefore, from this standpoint, it doesn't matter if you have been going to church for years or
for a few weeks, or whether you have never set

foot inside a church door before; whether you believe in God or are religious in some measure is a total irrelevance according to this teaching. If you are going to know God and receive eternal life, you *have* to be born again.

But how? How can this supernatural work take place in us? How can we be sure that we are real believers, and not like Nicodemus who merely thought he was? To answer that question Jesus uses an illustration which plays on a pun, for in Greek and Hebrew the word for Spirit and wind is the same – pneuma/ruach: *'The wind blows wherever it pleases. You hear its sound, but you cannot tell where it comes from or where it is going. So it is with everyone born of the Spirit'* (3:8).

'Look,' says Jesus in effect, 'you understand the wind, don't you? No, of course you don't. In fact, you haven't a clue where the wind comes from or where it is going to, but you believe in it. And the reason you believe in the wind is not because you can see it directly, but because you are aware of its effects – the blowing of the leaves, the scudding of clouds across the sky, feeling the breeze on your face. So it is with God's Spirit; you can't see him, but you can observe his effects.'

When someone for whom the name Jesus Christ was nothing more than a swear word becomes a person who loves him and serves him,

that is because they have been born again. When
the Bible becomes God speaking to a person, who
sits riveted when it is explained, such do so because they have been born again. When someone
for whom church was a deadly chore, turning up
because their parents told them they must, now
looks forward to going, the reason they do so is
because they have been born again. God has given
them new natures – new desires, new priorities.

But the reverse is also true. If coming to meet
with God and his people is something you do under sufferance or just when it happens to suit you,
then the Bible would have you question whether
you have been born again, however much you may
call yourself a Christian. If your eyes glaze over
at the beginning of a sermon, or you close your
Bibles and minds after fifteen minutes of a Christian talk (allowing that the speaker is mildly interesting!), then you have cause to wonder whether
you have been born again. Notice how Jesus said:
'You *must* be born again'. This is no option, it's a
necessity.

The method is in the message
'But how can this be?' asks Nicodemus in verse
9, 'How does it become a reality?'

The answer is that one pays close attention to
Jesus' teaching about the way of salvation (verses
11-14): 'I tell you the truth, we speak of what we

know, but you still don't accept it – you think you know it all. I have spoken to you about earthly things and even that is lost on you, even though you are an intellectual. So how are you going to respond when I start telling you about heavenly things, spiritual truths? I am well qualified to do that,' says Jesus, 'for I am not just a teacher, or a prophet, as you have wrongly assessed me, Nicodemus; I come from heaven. And why did I come? Not only to bring revelation, but salvation, rescue from your sins and certain judgment. Just as Moses lifted up the snake in the desert, so I, the Son of Man, must be lifted up on a cross, so that everyone who believes in me may have eternal life.'

Jesus has in mind an incident recorded in Numbers 21, when the Israelites were in the wilderness and they rebelled against God. The result was that in judgment God sent upon them a plague of poisonous snakes. But being a God of mercy as well as a God of justice, he told Moses to make a bronze snake and to put it on a pole so that when people looked to this in faith, they were healed of their snake bites. Some believed this, looked and lived. Others didn't and died. Those Israelites could not have understood how looking at a bronze snake could save them. They just had to take Moses' word for it.

It is the same with being saved from God's future judgment and its consequences, which the

Bible calls hell. We may not fully understand how
Jesus dying on the cross and taking our punish-
ment means that we can be forgiven and welcomed
as God's children, we just have to take his word
for it. But when we do, we find it works.

Jesus is saying to Nicodemus and to us, that
the question we should be asking is not, 'How
can this be?', but *'Who* can this be? *Who* is Jesus?'
You may be reading this with a mind crammed
full of objections: 'I can't believe in a God who
allows suffering', 'I can't believe in a God who
allows people to go to hell', 'I can't believe in
miracles', 'I can't believe ...'. If that is your position, then the affinity you have with Nicodemus
is striking; that is how he reacted.

The problem is that if you persist like that then
you will never make any progress. The doubts only
start to be answered substantially when you take
that step of personal faith, trusting that Jesus is
the Son of God who became man and died to put
you right with God. It is not until you are born
again that you will ever begin fully to understand
the Christian faith.

And maybe that is why it has been a mystery
to you until now, perhaps going along to the oc-
casional Christian meeting, flicking through the
odd Christian book, but never realizing that God
is calling you to make a personal response of the
whole of your life to a personal Christ. Look at

verse 16: *God so loved the world that he gave his one and only Son, that whoever believes in him shall not perish but have eternal life.* 'Your eternal destiny', says Jesus, 'turns on how you respond to me.'

With a single exception, God will forgive a person absolutely anything. Whatever is on your conscience God will forgive it. He loves the world and he does not want you to perish – he really doesn't. So much so that he sent his one and only Son to die for people like you and me.

But, according to verse 18, the one thing God will not forgive is the rejection of that gift of eternal life which he offers in the person of his Son: *'Whoever does not believe stands condemned already because he has not believed in the name of God's one and only Son.'*

Excuses, excuses

We all have our excuses for not considering the claims of Christ seriously and some may be covered with high-sounding respectable terms like 'agnosticism' or 'atheism'. But whatever they may be and however sincerely they may be held, Jesus, I am sure, would want to question them. If he can confront a professor like Nicodemus about the sincerity of his beliefs, he can do it with you and me.

Jesus insists that the *real* reason for people not

believing in him and surrendering their lives to
him is because, as the account says in verse 20,
they actually prefer spiritual darkness rather than
light. To be a Christian will mean a big change,
especially in our priorities, so that God and worship of him come first instead of self, and, if the
truth be known, many feel it is all too much. That
is why Jesus insists that the fundamental reason
such cannot see the light is because deep down
they don't want to see it. If people are ignorant it
is a culpable ignorance.

I well remember having to eat humble pie and
admit that was the plain truth about me; I knew
about Christianity, I saw what a difference it made
in the lives of others, intellectually I couldn't deny
it was true. But I wouldn't let it affect me, because I thought that I was so important and self-
sufficient that no-one, not even God, was going
to tell me how I was going to run my life. For all
that to change *I* had to be 'born again'.

'But,' you say, 'I am a good person.' So was
Nicodemus. You claim, 'I believe in God,' so did
Nicodemus. You protest, 'I go to church,' so did
Nicodemus. But Jesus would say to you now as
he said to Nicodemus then, if you want to be forgiven and receive a new inner nature with the sure
prospect of eternal life, then you must stop making excuses, trust in his death and resurrection
and ask him to rule over your life.

3

Jesus meets a sceptic
(John 1:30-51)

Communicating with people is not always as easy as it may first appear. For example, a few years ago the American cola firm *Pepsi* launched a major sales campaign in China, running the advertisement: '*Pepsi* makes you come alive.' To their surprise, not to say profound disappointment, the sale of *Pepsi Cola* in that country plummeted to an all-time low. An investigation was launched immediately to trace the cause of this disaster. What was the problem? The problem lay in the translation which read literally: '*Pepsi* makes your ancestors come back from the dead'. Presumably the Chinese weren't too keen on meeting some of their dead relatives!

Has it ever struck you how effective Jesus and his followers were in communicating with those around them? How, far from relying on slick advertising campaigns, the emphasis was very much on personal contact? We see something of this remarkable phenomenon in the biblical passage which is the focus of this chapter. It tells the story

33

of how, through some very effective communicating, a sceptic called Nathanael became a believer.

The next day John [the Baptist] was there again with two of his disciples. When he saw Jesus passing by, he said, 'Look, the Lamb of God!'

When the two disciples heard him say this, they followed Jesus. Turning round, Jesus saw them following and asked, 'What do you want?'

They said, 'Rabbi' (which means teacher), 'where are you staying?'

'Come,' he replied, 'and you will see.'

So they went and saw where he was staying, and spent that day with him. It was about the tenth hour.

Andrew, Simon Peter's brother, was one of the two who heard what John had said and who had followed Jesus. The first thing Andrew did was to find his brother Simon and tell him, 'We have found the Messiah' (that is, the Christ).

And he brought Simon to Jesus who looked at him and said, 'You are Simon son of John. You will be called Cephas' (which, when translated, is Peter).

The next day Jesus decided to leave for Galilee. Finding Philip, he said to him, 'Follow me.'

Philip, like Andrew and Peter, was from the town of Bethsaida. Philip found Nathanael and told him, 'We have found the one Moses wrote

*about in the Law, and about whom the prophets
also wrote – Jesus of Nazareth, the son of Joseph.'*

*'Nazareth! Can anything good come from
there?' Nathanael asked* (1:35-46).

A pattern to follow

Verse 43 could be translated: The next day *he* decided to go to Galilee. *He* found Philip and Jesus
said to him, 'Come, follow me.' The 'he' is in
fact Andrew, who is last mentioned in verse 40. If
this is so, then the pattern which runs throughout
this passage, and which Christians are to follow,
is of someone coming into contact with Jesus
Christ and being so taken by that encounter, he or
she in turn goes out and brings someone else along
to meet him.

Thus, in verse 36 we have John the Baptist seeing Jesus, pointing people to him and saying,
'Behold the Lamb of God.' Totally intrigued by
this announcement, two men start stalking Jesus,
wanting to discover where he lives so that they
can find out more. This they do, only to spend the
whole day in conversation with him. And what a
time that must have been, because the first thing
one of them – Andrew – does, is to seek out his
brother Simon and tell him that they have found
the promised Messiah and introduces him
accordingly. Still eager because of his new find,
Andrew descends upon his friend Philip, who in

turn passes on the news to Nathanael.

This method of one person telling another person, who tells another, is how the church grew then and how it grows today. In fact, this is what the Bible means by the term 'witnessing to Christ' – Christians making and taking the opportunity to tell others very simply who Jesus is, what he has done, and how they can become Christians too. You don't particularly have to be an extrovert or well versed in academic theology to do this. All that is required is a personal experience of Christ as your Lord and Saviour, and a willingness to be used by him as his mouthpiece.

The problem facing most Christians is not so much being willing to tell others about the Christian faith, but feeling able. Once the relationship with someone has been established, just how do you turn the conversation around in a natural fashion to speak of Christian things?

In his useful book *Know and Tell the Gospel*[1] the Australian evangelist John Chapman gives some very helpful advice on how we might proceed.

For example, he writes that if the man next to you at work tells you that his wife has cancer, you may say something like: 'You must be terribly

---

1. John Chapman, *Know and Tell the Gospel*, Hodder and Stoughton, 1987, pages 101-102

worried. My wife and I go to a prayer group on Tuesdays. Would you mind if we prayed for you both?' Or when asked, 'What sort of weekend did you have?' instead of saying, 'Oh, it was alright', try: 'We heard a terrific sermon on Sunday night' and see where it leads.

He then gives an ordinary example of a conversation he had with a neighbour one night as he was putting out the dustbins.

The neighbour pointed out that vandals had chopped down several shrubs in the park opposite and he was very angry about it. John Chapman could have said, 'Yes, terrible isn't it – young people these days, what can you do with them!' and then made a tactful withdrawal. But he didn't. Instead the conversation went something like this:

'What a hopeless action that is,' the neighbour said, referring to the damaged trees.

'We had better get used to it,' replied Chapman. 'I suspect it will get worse, not better.'

'That's a fairly pessimistic view,' said the neighbour.

'It's inevitable when you say goodbye to God,' said Chapman. 'It is difficult to teach people not to give full expression to anything they want to do.'

'I don't believe in God and I don't chop down trees,' replied the irate neighbour.

To which Chapman asked, 'Why shouldn't a

person do it if he feels like it?'

'Because the rest of us cannot enjoy them,' said the neighbour.

'But why should that worry us?' Chapman pressed.

'Because that is how we ought to live,' pleaded the neighbour.

'Who says so?' queried Chapman, 'I agree with you, but I do so because God says so. But if it's just a matter of your opinion plus my opinion versus the vandal's opinion, I can't see why ours is right and his is wrong. Only God is able to make statements about what is ultimately right and wrong.'

From there the conversation moved on to talk about the existence of God and the person of Jesus Christ. All that came about as a result of vandalism in the local park!

But you may say, 'We have tried. I have prayed for opportunities. I have even spoken to folk about Christ and invited them along to hear the gospel, but it has been met with nothing but stubborn resistance.' If that is so, then this passage encourages us not to lose heart, for the response of Nathanael wasn't initially encouraging either.

Full of enthusiasm, Philip tells Nathanael about the greatest discovery any Jew could have made – the discovery of the Messiah, Jesus of Nazareth. But what of Nathanael?

'Nazareth! Can anything good come from there?' Nathanael asked.

'Come and see,' said Philip (1:46).

How do you think Philip felt? Disappointed? Put off? Disappointed maybe, but certainly not discouraged. 'Look', he says in effect, 'come and see for yourself. You don't simply have to take my word for it, do your own investigating and make up your own mind.'

Surely that is a fair and reasonable response? Gently saying to people, 'I can lend you a little booklet explaining what Christians believe. Why not read John's Gospel and, if it will help, I can read it with you.'

What's the problem?

Why was Nathanael, like many people today, so sceptical about Jesus? There are two reasons.

First, Nathanael was one of those people who knew his Bible, more specifically his Old Testament. As far as he was concerned there was no mention in it of God's special messenger, the Messiah, coming from the despised, northern town of Nazareth. However, had he known that Jesus had in fact been born in Bethlehem, he may have been more open, because that was King David's town, and the prophecies were crystal clear on that point – that is where the Christ was going to come from. But Nazareth! Why the very suggestion was so ludicrous that it couldn't be taken seriously.

Secondly, everyone knew that nothing but trouble came from Nazareth; it had a reputation for being a hotbed of political subversives and religious cranks. Therefore, it was not surprising that to Nathanael's way of thinking Philip had stumbled across one of these folk who, if they were around today, might belong to the 'Monster Raving Loony Party'. The result: Nathanael was sceptical.

It may be that you too feel the same: 'Jesus – just another prophet at best, or a confidence trickster at worst. After all, the church is full of them, look at those TV evangelists for example. Christianity! That is nothing but opiate for the masses, fairy-tale stuff for the weak-minded.'

If you think that, I can only sympathize with you; at one time I thought like that too.

But notice something very important about Nathanael; he didn't allow his prejudice and scepticism to get in the way of finding out the truth. He had the courage and humility to take up Philip's offer and find out for himself.

When Jesus saw Nathanael approaching, he said of him, 'Here is a true Israelite, in whom there is nothing false.'

'How do you know me?' Nathanael asked.

Jesus answered, 'I saw you while you were still under the fig-tree before Philip called you' (1:47-48).

An attitude to praise

Jesus recognized the integrity of the man. He wasn't a hypocrite, but someone who was sincere in his quest for the truth, not using his religious background as a mask for ulterior motives. Today we would describe him as 'dead straight'.

This is an attitude which God honours, as the words of Jesus indicate. If you are serious in meaning business with God, and not just throwing up smokescreens to hide from God, forever asking the 'What about ... questions': 'What about suffering? What about other religions?' and so on, then God will honour you and you will find him. That is the type of God he is.

What was it that turned this sceptic into a believer, a true follower of Christ? It was the coming together of two things – what the Bible taught and what experience confirmed.

First, what the Bible taught. This was something that Philip had picked up: *'We have found the one Moses wrote about in the Law, and about whom the prophets also wrote'* (1:45). Probably one of the passages he had in mind was Deuteronomy 18, where we read that God would send a prophet like Moses whom the people were to obey. Also there is a whole host of other passages which point to Jesus (e.g. Psalm 22; Psalm 110; Isaiah 53; Ezekiel 37; Malachi 4). Nathanael knew his Bible too, and this may have lain behind Jesus' comment that he saw Nathanael 'under the fig-tree', which in that culture would have been an ideal place to sit to read and meditate upon the Scriptures.

But the force of this truth, that Jesus was not just a prophet but *the* prophet, God's own Son, was brought home to Nathanael personally by the prophetic insight Jesus displayed, thus his experience confirmed the witness of the Scriptures.

Jesus began by assessing Nathanael's character perfectly: *'Here is a true Israelite, in whom there is nothing false'*, which prompted Nathanael to ask: *'How do you know me?'* as they had never met before (verses 47-48). What was to follow punctured his sceptical armour irrevocably. It was what could only be called supernatural knowledge, for Jesus *knew* that miles away Nathanael had been sitting under a fig-tree. How else do you explain that, save that Jesus is someone very special indeed? Here we see how the testimony of Scripture on the one hand, combined with a personal encounter on the other, led to Nathanael's conversion, to Nathanael recognizing that he was standing face to face with none other than God's appointed King.

Then Nathanael declared, 'Rabbi, you are the Son of God; you are the King of Israel' (1:49).

The same is true today. What brings people to faith? It is the truth of the Word of God applied directly and personally to people's lives. We are never to underestimate the power of the Bible in the hands of its author, the Holy Spirit, to change hearts and minds, even the most sceptical.

A promise to receive

What is more, for those like Nathanael who are willing to put their prejudices to one side and consider for themselves the claims of Christ, there is a promise to be received: *Jesus said: 'You believe because I told you I saw you under the fig-tree. You shall see greater things than that.' He then added, 'I tell you the truth, you shall see heaven open, and the angels of God ascending and descending on the Son of Man'* (1:50-51). What does Jesus mean by this cryptic remark?

He has in mind the story of Jacob, recorded in Genesis 28, which relates the dream Jacob had of a ladder reaching up to heaven with angels going up and coming down and God standing beside him. Jacob accordingly named the place 'Bethel', which means 'God's dwelling place'.

With this incident in mind (which may well have been the passage Nathanael had been contemplating under the fig-tree) Jesus was saying to him: 'Do you remember from your reading of the Scriptures under the fig-tree how Jacob found a doorway to heaven? Well, you have found a new doorway, and that doorway is me. Just as Jacob came into the presence of God, you too have come into God's presence, in me. What is more, just as Bethel was the point of contact between heaven and earth, between God and man, I am the new point of contact. Do you want to know God, Nathanael? Do you want to have direct access into the very portals of heaven? Then look no further, for all these things are fulfilled in me.' The result? Nathanael's life was turned right round.

Is it that simple? In many ways, yes.

Listen to someone who discovered this for himself. A former UVF terrorist in Northern Ireland, David Hamilton relates how he was arrested on charges of terrorism, became a Christian in prison, and like Philip and Nathanael went on to introduce others to Jesus Christ. [2]

'The police raided my house in the early hours of the morning, and I was arrested, and spent a year in prison waiting for my trial. When I went to court I received a total of 44 years.

'On the day that I was sentenced my mother called in to my uncle's house on her way home, to tell him the news. My mother was crying and very upset, and she said, "You know, there's no hope for my son because he is just caught up in this violence, and even if he was out of prison he would

---

2. Extracts from a testimony related in *Evangelicals Now*, February 1994.

be involved again. This is his third prison sentence, and he will never change. He's just a hopeless case."

'But there was an old lady sitting there in my uncle's house. She was 83 years of age. She said to my mother, "That's not true. God can change your son." My mother just smiled and thanked her. She didn't really believe there was much chance of that happening. But this old lady was able to tell my mother that she would pray for me every day that God would change my heart.

'Fourteen months later I was sitting in my prison cell and drinking a cup of tea. There was a Christian tract on my bed. I remember thinking it was disgusting and I threw it out of the window. I went to church as a child. I just thought I had no time for all this nonsense. Prison was bad, but church was worse!

'I sat on my bed drinking tea, and there came this thought at the back of my mind to become a Christian. I thought: "This is terrible. Someone has put dope in my tea. Why am I thinking like this?"

'I remember looking up at the shelf and seeing the Bible. There was a Bible in every cell thanks to the Gideons. I thought: "Even if I wanted to be a Christian, God would say: 'Not you, you're too bad, it is only for nice people or good people.' God wouldn't be interested in me anyway even if I wanted to be a Christian."

'I lifted the Bible down and started to read some verses out of the fly-pages – where you find help, etc. I looked at some of these and read "For God so loved the world ..." I thought: "That means good people, it doesn't mean the bad people." I put the Bible back up because I thought God wouldn't be interested.

'Then God showed me something I'd never seen before. He showed me that he'd kept me alive. The IRA had tried to kill me several times. As I sat on the bed I thought: "Why can't God not be interested in me if he's kept me alive?"

'The next day I decided. I said: "God, I know you're real, but if you are interested in me, take away the violence and the bitterness I have, and change me, because I want to make sure that it does change me."

'I prayed that prayer on my knees on January 29 1980. I asked the Lord Jesus to save me. God changed me that day. I began to read the Word of God and I can honestly say my life changed. That day I stopped smoking, stopped taking dope, stopped drinking – everything changed.

'After that I led IRA men to the Lord, sex offenders to the Lord and many other men too. God showed me: "Don't be looking down at others because God loves sinners." God showed me grace in my life.'

David Hamilton is not unique; many a sceptic

has turned believer. The invitation of the psalmist still stands: 'Taste and see that the LORD is good' (Psalm 34:8). Have you tasted?

4

Jesus meets a wedding party
(John 2:1-11)

One of the most remarkable episodes of the Second World War, in many people's opinion, was the evacuation of the British troops from the beaches of Dunkirk when they were snatched from the jaws of the advancing German army. Without doubt the timing was remarkable, as were the weather conditions, together with the fact that Hitler had actually ordered the Panzer divisions to stop in their tracks. Not surprisingly, therefore, this is often referred to as the 'miracle' of Dunkirk.

Without wishing to deny for a moment that this was an amazing act of God's overruling providence and the answer to many prayers, that is not quite how the term 'miracle' is used in the Bible. In fact, more often than not it is terms such as 'signs' or 'wonders' that are used to describe extraordinary occurrences brought about by God to further his saving purposes in the world. We are not talking about 'magic', the sort of things which you might find in fairy stories or myths,

49

but unusual happenings which tie in perfectly with
the character and intentions of God himself.

Near the beginning of his work, John records
what he calls the 'first' of many miraculous signs,
which he takes to testify to who Jesus is and what
he came to do. And it occurred at a wedding.

The situation

*On the third day a wedding took place at Cana in
Galilee. Jesus' mother was there, and Jesus and
his disciples had also been invited to the wedding*
(2:1-2). On the face of it there is nothing extraordinary about the situation at all. It is a simple Jewish wedding party which could go on for about a
week. The fact that Jesus, his mother and his disciples were invited as guests would suggest that it
was the wedding of a close relative, with Mary
perhaps having some responsibility for the cater-
ing arrangements.

So here is this splendid occasion with friends
and relatives from all over the country celebrat-
ing the wedding of a nephew or niece, without a
care in the world; singing, dancing, catching up
on the latest gossip about shady Uncle Moshe,
when suddenly disaster strikes – the wine runs
out.

*When the wine was gone, Jesus' mother said
to him, 'They have no more wine.'*

'Dear woman, why do you involve me?' Jesus

replied, 'My time has not yet come' (2:3-4).

Why all the fuss? To answer that question we need to appreciate something of the Jewish culture at that time. In this setting, to run out of wine on such an occasion was the height of social embarrassment, designed to bring shame upon the host family which would be very difficult to live down.

What is more, since it was the bridegroom and not the bride's father who was responsible for the financing of the wedding, he was actually open to a lawsuit from the aggrieved relatives of the bride under the equivalent to our trades description act. Not exactly a promising start to married life! We may now appreciate a little more fully why there was so much concern and perhaps more than a hint of panic on the part of Mary when the news reached her that there was no more wine left.

Mary did what every good Jewish mother would do; she turned to her son: 'Look,' she said, 'they have no more wine'; with the implication, 'What are you going to do about it?'

There is no indication at this stage that Mary expected Jesus to perform a miracle, after all, in verse 11 we are told that this was the first of Jesus' miraculous signs, so she had no precedent to rely on. Maybe she simply expected Jesus to try to rustle up some cheap wine from a friend in the neighbourhood in the hope of saving the day.

The fact that Mary's concerns were restricted to purely worldly concerns – saving a social event – is underscored by Jesus' response in verse 4: *'Dear woman, why do you involve me?'* Or, as it could be translated, 'Your concerns are not my concerns.' In other words, 'The priorities you have are not shared by me.'

What are Jesus' priorities? These are indicated by the second part of his response in verse 4: *'My time or hour has not yet come.'* What does Jesus mean by that?

Throughout John's Gospel, Jesus' 'hour' refers to his crucifixion, culminating in his resurrection and ascension (e.g. 16:32). In other words, his primary purpose on earth is to bring men and women back to God, giving them eternal life through the forgiveness of their sins by him dying in their place on the cross. That is Jesus' concern. That is his priority, and everything else has to take second place. Therefore, in these words to Mary we do find a gentle rebuke that even she may put first things first.

Right at the beginning of his ministry, Jesus makes clear his utter freedom from human advice and human priorities, however good these may be, in order that he may not be distracted from his God-given task of bringing people to himself. As Christians we need to pause and take stock of this rebuke by Jesus and ask to what extent it is a rebuke to us? Are our concerns Jesus' concerns? Think for a moment how easy it is for Christians to get worked up over so many trivial matters: whether the minister wears robes, whether a church should have pews or stained glass windows or choirs.

If only Christians would expend the same amount of concern and energy on things that really matter to Christ, such as the evangelization of the world. At the very least, Christians should be concerned about these other things for the right reasons. So we may need to ask: are robes or pews or services a help in reaching the outsider or a hindrance? Will these things promote the kingdom of God or not, or are they a matter of sheer indifference? Do you see how with Christ we are to evaluate everything by this one test – will the gospel be promoted and God glorified?

Following on from Jesus' gentle rebuke a wonderful change occurs in Mary. She takes the rebuke to heart; she doesn't allow it to get her down, brooding about it or resenting it. In fact, she exemplifies the best kind of persevering faith – she is content to leave matters in the capable hands of Jesus.

His mother said to the servants, 'Do whatever he tells you' (2:5).

That is what the Bible calls faith, a faith which leads to obedience, letting God be God so that he does things in his own way and in his own time. Mary approaches Jesus as his mother, presuming upon family ties and is reproached, but then she responds as a believer and her faith is honoured. That is precisely the response Jesus looks for in us.

The sign

Nearby stood six stone water jars, the kind used by the Jews for ceremonial washing, each holding from twenty to thirty gallons.

Jesus said to the servants, 'Fill the jars with water'; so they filled them to the brim.

Then he told them, 'Now draw some water out and take it to the master of the banquet.'

They did so, and the master of the banquet tasted the water that had been turned into wine. He did not realise where it had come from, though the servants who had drawn the water knew (2:6-9).

In the middle of a crisis when people need wine, Jesus directs them to get water. What a seemingly strange thing to do. 'What is the point in doing that, Jesus? It is wine we want, not water. Why, all that business of washing our hands to make us ceremonially clean has been done at the beginning of the party – we don't need to go through all that again.' Such would have been the thoughts running through the minds of the servants. Nonetheless, being good stewards they did as they were told.

However, you can be sure that the bewilderment didn't end there, for although traditionally it is assumed that it was the water in the stone jars that Jesus turned into wine, the original wording suggests a different interpretation, namely, that it was the water *drawn from the well,* after the stone jars had been filled, that became wine.[1] In other words, up to then the servants had been drawing up water to fill the jars used for ceremonial washing, they *now* draw up water which becomes wine for the feast. Given that the water comes from the well, it logically follows that the supply is endless, it is abundant.

What is more, if this were just any wine, that would be impressive enough as a miracle, but that it is the best wine possible places this miracle in a league of its own.

Then [the master] called the bridegroom aside and said, 'Everyone brings out the choice wine first and then the cheaper wine after the guests have had too much to drink; but you have saved the best till now' (2:10). Do you see how simple obedience to Jesus, even in what appears to be the most absurd task, can result in blessings beyond our wildest dreams?

---

1. The verb 'draw' (antleo, verse 8) is commonly used for drawing water from a well (as in John 4:7, 15). The word 'now' may also support this view.

Let me give an example of what I mean. Early one Saturday morning there were two sixth-form students waiting at a bus stop, chatting away to each other, when an old man came along. He asked the two lads which school they went to and what they hoped to do when they left. He then asked them, 'Do either of you go to church?' Half embarrassed, but with a bit of bravado they said no, they didn't believe in that sort of thing. They were studying science, they said, and it was well known that scientists were sceptical when it came to matters of religion. Then the old man went on to say that he hoped they didn't mind, but he felt it was important that he told them why he was a Christian, because if he didn't he would have been worse than a thief, taking something from them which was theirs by right.

The two lads listened to what he had to say, gave up waiting for the bus, and walked off. As far as that old man was concerned, they were just another two teenagers who didn't want to know. But what he could not know was that one of those teenagers had already started to think about the Christian faith, and what the old man said really impressed him. That former teenager is the one who wrote this book.

Do whatever Jesus tells you, and be surprised at the results. A little obedience can go a long way in God's hands.

The significance

On the face of it, there was nothing extraordinary at all. But when you look a little beneath the surface with the eyes of faith, you soon discover that at every conceivable level everything in this story is shot through with the most amazing significance – nothing is quite as it seems.

First, we have the timing; John notes that it was the third day when all of this took place. When you work this backwards to take into account the events recorded in John 1, it means that this event occurred at the end of a whole week of the most extraordinary activity. In other words, it happened on the seventh day. [2]

For those who have more than a passing acquaintance with the Bible, the seventh day is,

---

2. This dating is argued by D A Carson in his *The Gospel According to St John*, IVP, 1991, Pages 167-168. Thus
Day 1: a delegation is sent to John the Baptist (1:19-28)
Day 2: John announces Jesus as the Lamb of God (1:29)
Day 3: the two disciples seek out Jesus (1:35-42)
Day 4: the Nathaniel incident
The wedding took place 'the third day' after that (inclusively two days later). When another day is added by virtue of the fact that when the Baptist's two disciples attach themselves to Jesus, it is already 4pm on the third day and they spend the rest of the day with him. Andrew introduces Simon Peter on the next day (the fourth), Nathaniel's exchange occurs on the fifth day, the changing of water into wine on the seventh.

of course, brimful of significance, marking the day when God stood back, as it were, from the creation he had just made and pronounced it good. Here we have Jesus, the one who brings about God's new creation, a whole new relationship with God, symbolized by the miracle of the new and best wine God freely gives to those who trust him.

It was also the Sabbath, God's rest. What is the true Sabbath to which the earthly Sabbath is but a pointer? It is the rest – peace – with God which comes through salvation in Jesus Christ, a peace which we can know now, but which we shall experience fully only in heaven. (Read chapter 4 of the Letter to the Hebrews.) The very timing of this miracle speaks of a new start, a new peace which Christ alone can give.

But what of the occasion? It is a wedding and that is no accident either. It is at a wedding of all events that we see the culmination of God's creation in which his divine image finds expression, echoing Genesis 1:27: 'God created man in his own image, in the image of God he created him, male and female he created them.' So what better occasion than at a wedding to perform the first and primary miracle which points to God's new work in Jesus Christ whereby that image marred by sin begins to be restored?

But there is even more to it than that. Jesus often likened his relationship to his followers, the church, as a bridegroom to a bride. He is the one who has come into the world to create and save his bride, the church he loves, by dying for her, so that one day, in the great wedding reception of heaven, she may be presented before God as the most beautiful and radiant creature the universe has ever seen – pure, holy, obediently in love with her Lord, who is none other than Jesus himself.

However, there is a significance in the miracle itself, a significance which is heightened, by way of contrast, with the filling of the Jewish ceremonial stone jars with water. Why did Jesus order that to be done? It was to make a very important point. You see, by filling the jars to the brim, so that nothing more could be added, in effect he was declaring that the old order of Jewish law and custom was now coming to an end and was about to be replaced by something infinitely better; the new wine of God's kingdom.

In the Old Testament, prophets like Jeremiah (31:12), Hosea (14:7) and Amos (9:13-14) characterized the coming age of the Messiah as a time when wine would flow freely, a time of rejoicing and celebration. That is what Christ came to bring. There is nothing dull about true Christianity; quite the opposite.

Jewish ceremonial could take people only so far. All that business of ceremonial washing could literally only cleanse the outside of a person; it could not change people inside. But as a pointer to that which was to come, it did serve as a visual aid of what the Christ would do – namely, make people inwardly clean by washing away their sin, and replacing a life of insipid legalism with a life in which God would be known personally through his Son by his Spirit.

The real tragedy, however, is that whilst Christ offers a new life which is more refreshing than the best possible wine, people will insist on going back to the water of ceremonial religion. Jesus as our high priest came to abolish the Jewish system of priests and replace it with the priesthood of all believers and the office of pastor-teacher. Yet what we find happening today is that certain sections of the church are introducing a new priesthood and turning the table of the Lord's supper into an altar for a sacrifice. Instead of a personal relationship with Christ which affects every area of our lives throughout the week, the tendency is still for church-going, with folk doing their bit of religion when occasion demands.

When Jesus had those ceremonial jars filled to the brim, he marked once and for all the end of that sort of religion. We are not meant to replace it with a Christianized version of Judaism, bound by our own little rituals and ceremonies, no matter how hallowed by time and tradition they may be. Christ is the reality, so everything we sing, say or do must point to him and what he has done, and not eclipse him. When our traditions become more important than Christ, then it is as if we are going back to those ceremonial vessels.

The Danish writer Soren Kierkegaard once made this very astute observation: 'Whereas Christ turned water into wine, the church has done something far more remarkable – it has turned wine into water.' The wine of the gospel, the wonderful news that men and women can be forgiven by God and come to know him for all eternity, as they repent and put their trust in him, has been so diluted by moralism, or ceremonialism, or theological liberalism, that it is hardly recognizable as biblical at all.

What we have to grasp is that all of the signs – miracles – Jesus performed and which are recorded by John, are not ends in themselves but means to an end; a means of leading people to faith in Christ.

This, the first of his miraculous signs, Jesus performed in Cana of Galilee. He thus revealed his glory, and his disciples put their faith in him (2:11).

These are not odd happenings of the Uri Geller variety, the first-century equivalent to spoon bending; they are visual messages packed with meaning, which force us to ask: 'Who is this doing such things?' When we ask that question and look very carefully at what Jesus does, together with what he says, then we can come to no other reasonable conclusion than that this man is also God, doing the sort of things we would expect only God to do. Therefore, the response it calls for from us is the surrender of the whole of our lives to him.

It is in that self-surrender that we actually taste the new wine of God's rule which Christ came to bring. But it is only that, a taste, the full enjoyment awaits us at the end of time when those who trust in Christ will find themselves at another wedding party – the marriage supper of the Lamb.

5

Jesus meets a social outcast
(John 4:1-41)

'Would you tell me please which way I ought to go from here?' asked Alice. 'That depends a good deal on where you want to go,' said the Cat. 'I don't much care where ...' said Alice. 'Then it doesn't much matter which way you go,' replied the Cat.[1]

She was a woman of the world. A hardened veteran of life. Some called her a hussy – shameless. Others simply pitied her. Not that she wanted their pity. She just wanted to be left alone, left to get on with her life her own way. Sure, she had been hurt. But not any more. By a masterful combination of cynicism and social manoeuvring, she had developed some very effective means of self-protection. She didn't much care where her life was heading and therefore it did not seem to matter that much which way she should go. That is, until she met the stranger who asked her, *her*, of all people for a drink.

---

1. Lewis Carroll's, *Alice Through the Looking Glass*

Who was the stranger? The stranger was Jesus and we read about this amazing encounter with a social outcast in John chapter 4.

Overcoming the divide

Now he (Jesus) had to go through Samaria. So he came to a town in Samaria called Sychar, near the plot of ground Jacob had given to his son Joseph. Jacob's well was there, and Jesus, tired as he was from the journey, sat down by the well. It was about the sixth hour (verses 4-9).

When a Samaritan woman came to draw water, ·Jesus said to her, 'Will you give me a drink?' (His disciples had gone into the town to buy food.)

The Samaritan woman said to him, 'You are a Jew and I am a Samaritan woman. How can you ask me for a drink?' (For Jews do not associate with Samaritans.)

Xenophobia, the fear, and in some cases, the hatred of foreigners is not a modern phenomenon. It existed in Jesus' day, right here in fact, in Samaria. Like so many such feelings which appeared to border on the irrational, its roots lay deep in history. The problem began in 720 BC, when the Assyrians conquered the northern kingdom of Samaria, and encouraged widespread immigration from Babylon and other countries (2 Kings 17:24).

Almost inevitably there followed the intermarrying between Samaritan Jews and immigrants. After the exile, Jews returning to their homeland, which was the remains of the southern kingdom, looked upon Samaritans not only as children of political rebels (as if that were not bad enough) but as racial and religious half-breeds. Add the fact that in 400 BC the Samaritans erected a rival temple on Mount Gerizim which was then destroyed by John Hyracanus the ruler of Judea, and you have all the ingredients for a recipe of deep hatred and mistrust which would run for generations to come. To make matters worse, in AD 6 some Samaritans broke into the Jerusalem temple at night and scattered human bones there, so defiling the sacred place just before a Jewish feast – not exactly the best way to win friends and influence people! What is more the Samaritans had developed their own religious traditions based solely upon the first five books of the Hebrew Bible – the Pentateuch, the rest was not considered authoritative. By the time of Jesus, the gulf between Jews and Samaritans had been irretrievably fixed and had taken on cavernous proportions.

It was into such a seething cauldron of religious and racial hatred that Jesus deliberately walked on that hot sunny afternoon as, tired and thirsty, he stopped by a well.

Strange though it may seem for a Jew to find himself alone in the Samaritan heartland, stranger

still was the sight of a woman going alone at
midday to draw water from a well. Normally the
women of the village would travel together and
certainly would avoid the searing noonday sun. In
what was already a strange and potentially volatile
situation Jesus uttered the words: 'Will you give
me a drink?'

What is the response of the woman to this
seemingly innocent request? It is to lay down her
first layer of defence – a cynical rebuffal, 'You are
a Jew and I am a Samaritan woman. How can you
ask me for a drink?' (For Jews do not associate
with Samaritans – or as it can be translated 'Jews
do not use dishes Samaritans have used', that
would make them ritually unclean by contamina-
tion). The scholar John Calvin suggests that the
woman's words might be interpreted in the following manner, 'Oh! You're sure it's all right to
ask me for a drink, when you think we are so
irreligious'. Centuries of prejudice and hatred
immediately erupted to the surface.

But there may have been far more which lay
behind this cutting response. As becomes apparent later in the story, the woman may have had
something of a reputation for being 'loose'. She
would be familiar with the 'chat up' line of men,
men who would have considered her easy game.
And so she may have suspected such motives of
Jesus. Why else should he a Jew be asking such a

favour of her? Did not their own rabbis have a saying: 'A man should not salute a woman in a public place, not even his own wife'? Hence the rebuttal to keep Jesus safe at arms length.

The gift

Notice how gracious and generous is Jesus' reply: *Jesus answered her, 'If you knew the gift of God and who it is that asks you for a drink, you would have asked him and he would have given you living water'* (verse 10).

Jesus refuses to respond in kind. Whatever misgivings she had about him, Jesus had no such misgivings about her. Whatever the religious or social taboos, Jesus is more than willing to break them down for the sake of the individual and the 'gift of God' he came to bring.

It is no accident that this story immediately follows on from that of Nicodemus, it acts as a suitable counterfoil which makes the same point. Nicodemus was a Jew, theologically trained, religiously orthodox, a male of aristocratic stock; she is untrained, a female peasant and religiously suspect. The contrast could not be greater. Yet Jesus engages with them both.

The same is true today. No matter what your background, no matter what your present state, Jesus will not allow barriers to get in the way of him addressing you. A minister friend of mine was

visiting his parishioners one day in a fairly well-
to-do area and was frequently being met with the
response 'I am not interested in Christianity or
Christ', to which he replied 'No doubt, but I want
you to know that Christ is very much interested in
you'. He is indeed, very interested. More to the
point we should be interested in what he has to
offer – 'Living water'.

This could be understood at two levels. Literally, it refers to fresh, running water from springs
– flowing water. Metaphorically, it speaks of the
grace and knowledge of God and the life trans-
forming power of the Holy Spirit (Isaiah 1:16-18;
Ezekiel 36:25-27). Through his prophet Jeremiah,
God had complained that his people had forsaken
him 'the spring of living water, and have dug their
own cisterns, broken cisterns that cannot hold
water.' Both the morally upright Nicodemus and
the morally dissolute woman have the same need
and Jesus offers the same remedy – the cleansing,
renewing power of God's Spirit (cf. 3:5). The
promises of God that the prophets looked forward
to, Jesus now provides.

Given the lack of familiarity of the woman with
the prophetic writings which were regarded by the
Samaritans as uncanonical, it is perhaps not surprising that she takes Jesus words solely at the first
level of meaning. *'Sir,' the woman said, 'you have
nothing to draw the water with and the well is*

deep. Where can you get this living water? Are you greater than our father Jacob ...? '(verse 11).

The irony is remarkable! The woman displays a double misunderstanding, first with regard to the fact that the living water Jesus speaks of is not to be obtained from an ordinary well, and second, yes he *is* greater than Jacob, as she is soon to discover to her utter astonishment.

A universal need

Not deterred by the barbed sarcasm of the woman, Jesus simply builds upon her misunderstanding to enable her to perceive the truth –

Jesus answered, 'Everyone who drinks this water will be thirsty again, but whoever drinks the water I give him will never thirst. Indeed, the water I give him will become in him a spring of water welling up to eternal life' (verses 13-14).

In saying this, Jesus is giving us insight into the human condition, the fact that deep down we have a spiritual thirst which nothing but God can satisfy. Several years ago, the Hollywood actress, Raquel Welch said these revealing words in an interview with a national newspaper:

'I had acquired everything I wanted, yet I was totally miserable ... I thought it was very peculiar that I had acquired everything I had wanted as a child – wealth, fame and accomplishment in my career ... I had beautiful children and a lifestyle that seemed terrific, yet I was totally and miserably unhappy. I found it very frightening that one could acquire all these things and still be so miserable' (*The Daily Express*, 1972).

Is such a feeling unique? Not really. It is fundamental to the human experience. Just as the pangs of hunger we feel in our stomach are a reminder that we are made for food, so the spiritual hunger we feel reminds us that we are made for God. The French philosopher, Blase Pascal, reflecting on this phenomenon summarises his analysis in these words:

'What does all this restlessness and helplessness indicate, except that man was once in true happiness which has now left him? So he vainly searches, but finds nothing to help him, other than to see an infinite abyss that can only be filled by One who is Infinite and Immutable. In other words, it can only be filled by God himself.'[2]

That is what in effect Jesus is describing here,

2.*The Mind on Fire,* Blase Pascal, Edited by James Houston, Hodder and Stoughton, 1989, p109.

the very presence of God by his Spirit which is like a clear freshwater spring bubbling up from within to eternal life. That is what he offers.

The heart of the problem

The woman said to him, 'Sir, give me this water so that I won't get thirsty and have to keep coming here to draw water' (verse 15).

Still not going beyond the naturalistic plane, the woman lets slip a desire not to have to come to the well to collect water. Why such a concern? Is it simply that she is a little lazy, as if to say 'Chance would be a fine thing, what I wouldn't give to be spared the drudgery of lugging this pot backwards and forwards every day'? I think there is much more to it that. Something rather tragic. What that something is becomes apparent in the change of direction the conversation takes.

He told her, 'Go call your husband and come back.'

'I have no husband,' she replied.

Jesus said to her, 'You are right when you say you have no husband, the fact is, you have had five husbands, and the man you now have is not your husband. What you have just said is quite true' (verses 16-18).

That hurt. Jesus had touched a raw nerve. Whatever the circumstances which had led to her having had five husbands (whether through death or divorce) the fact is the man she is now living with is not her husband. No matter how morally inferior the Jews may have considered the Samaritans to have been, they were not so morally dissolute as to permit common law marriages; after all they still had the five books of Moses and that point was clear.

Now we may begin to understand why the woman was by herself at the well when normally the women from the village would have drawn water together, the well being a focal point for conversation and social discourse. The other women would treat her as a moral leper, a social outcast. No doubt she had been the subject of many a juicy morsel of gossip. The disdainful looks, the sneers would have become all too much for her and so she adopted her second line of self-protection – voluntary social isolation, collecting water at midday when no one else was around, thus sparing herself more pain. But the mere fact that she had to go to the well only served to rub further salt into the wound. That well was a perpetual reminder of her estrangement, her uncleanness, her failed relationships. Little wonder, therefore, that she wistfully longed to be able to obtain water some other way, a less painful way.

   'Sir,' the woman said, 'I can see that you are a prophet. Our fathers worshipped on this mountain, but you Jews claim that the place where we

must worship is in Jerusalem' (verse 19).

Some commentators have taken the woman's sudden interest in 'religion' as an attempt to deflect Jesus from probing any further in what was for her a very sensitive area. While it is true that a common ploy we adopt when God's Word is getting too close for comfort is to raise red-herrings, it is not so obvious that this is the case here.

The perception that Jesus is a prophet is no doubt genuine, as we see from the woman's public testimony in verse 29, 'Come, see a man who told me everything I ever did.' What is more, the original allows for the translation 'Sir, I can see you are *the* prophet.' The Samaritans took what Deuteronomy 34:19 said seriously, 'no prophet has risen in Israel like Moses, whom the Lord knew face to face' and linked this with the promise of *the* coming prophet mentioned in Deuteronomy 18:15f, whom they referred to as the Taheb, 'the Restorer'.

If the light is dawning on the woman that this is the one promised then it is understandable that she raises the question about the nature of worship, especially if because of her way of life she is feeling guilty and alienated. How can someone like her get back in touch with God? How can she be restored? Perhaps the 'Restorer', the Taheb, can tell her. Indeed, he does, and the answer is not as she expects.

The real new age

*Jesus declared, 'Believe me, woman, a time is
coming when you will worship the Father neither
on this mountain nor in Jerusalem. You Samaritans worship what you do not know; we worship
what we do know, for salvation is from the Jews.
Yet a time is coming and has now come when the
true worshippers will worship the Father in spirit
and truth, for they are the kind of worshippers the
Father seeks. God is spirit, and his worshippers
must worship in spirit and in truth'* (verses 21-24).

'Listen very carefully,' says Jesus, 'there is no
point in having a prolonged debate about the
relative merits and demerits of worshipping in
these places because they are about to be obsolete,
that type of worship is soon to be replaced with
something far more profound and intimate – worshipping God as *Father*.

'Nonetheless, don't draw the wrong inferences,
that there is no significant difference between
Jews and Samaritans as far as knowing God is
concerned, for there is. This is not a matter of
racial prejudice, but religious fact. You Samaritans stand outside God's flow of revelation. What
revelation you have is incomplete, truncated,
whereas it has been filled out for the Jews by the
prophetic writings. The picture of God and his
saving purposes are much fuller. In this sense,
salvation is from the Jews.

'But that as it may be, from a practical standpoint it is an irrelevance, for now we are on the
threshold of a new era, a new age no less when
what matters is worshipping God in spirit and in
truth and that embraces Samaritans as well as
Jews. You can actually *know* God who is spirit.'

By speaking of God as 'spirit', Jesus is not
saying that he is one spirit amongst many, but that
he stands in contrast to that which is human (look
again at chapter 3:6). God is invisible, the giver of
life, indeed the giver of new life and unless he
chooses to make himself known we cannot know
him. Then how can he be known? Unless this is
explained, conveyed in some way by God himself,
he cannot be worshipped in spirit and certainly not
in truth which carries the idea of objective doctri-
nal content.

*The woman said, 'I know that Messiah (called
Christ) is coming. When he comes, he will explain
everything to us.'*

*Then Jesus declared, 'I who speak to you am
he'* (verse 25).

The key to true worship, true forgiveness, the
fresh start the woman had been hoping for was
standing right before her. Jesus is God's self-
expression, 'the truth' and therefore worship of
God must be Christ-centred. Jesus is the one who
dispenses the 'living water', God's Spirit, and so
is the one who enables us to worship God 'in

spirit' – therefore, worship is Spirit enabled. In
Jesus the Samaritan-Jewish divide simply col-
lapses as he reconciles them to each other and to
God. And it happened, the breaking down of
centuries of prejudice and suspicion was effected
by the risen Jesus through His Spirit as the gospel
was preached (Acts 8). Although that was still
very much future, the first seeds of that full recon-
ciliation which was to come were sown here, as
through this woman's declaration, not only with
her lips but her changed life, others came to
believe too.

A fresh start

*Leaving her water jar, the woman went back to the
town and said to the people, 'Come and see a man
who told me everything I ever did. Could this be
the Christ?' They came out of the town and made
their own way towards him* (verses 28-30).

*Many of the Samaritans from that town be-
lieved in him because of the woman's testimony,
'He told me everything I ever did.' So when the
Samaritans came to him, they urged him to stay
with them, and he stayed two days. And because of
his words many more became believers* (verse
39).

What a transformation! The little detail recorded by John, that she left her water jar, is so
significant. The very symbol of her emptiness was

abandoned at Jesus' feet, for she had found the living water. Far from avoiding the townfolk out of fear, her encounter with Jesus propels her to meet with them to share her faith.

Christ effects the same transformation today. One Christian counsellor related the time a client came in to see him and this is what she said:

'Before I came here, I was involved in a life of sexual fun and games and in a real sense I felt good. It was exciting. Since I have decided to truly commit myself to Christ, I've found that life has become a struggle. The worldly life was easier and happier than the Christian life. But I wouldn't go back for anything. There's no turning around. I've tasted reality. Painful though it sometimes is, I want more. It's what life is all about. For the first time in my life, I feel truly alive, tuned in, I'm together. It hurts like blazes, but it's worth it, because now I am a person.'[3]

Have you honestly tasted reality? Can you say that you are a person in the fullest sense? There is one who invites you to drink of 'living water' so that these things may be so.

---

3. *Effective Biblical Counselling*, Larry Crabb, Marshalls, 1977, p131.

6

Jesus meets a paralytic
(John 5:1-15)

The scorpion, being a poor swimmer, asked the turtle to carry him on his back across the river.

'Do you think I'm mad?' exclaimed the turtle. 'I know what you'll do. You'll sting me while I'm swimming and I'll drown.'

'My dear turtle,' laughed the scorpion, 'if I were to sting you, you would drown and I would go down with you. Now where's the logic in that?'

'You're right,' cried the turtle. 'Hop on.' And this he duly did. But halfway across the river the turtle felt one almighty sting.

As they both sank to the bottom, the turtle said in a resigned sort of way, 'Do you mind if I ask you something? You said there'd be no logic in you stinging me, so why did you do it?'

To which the drowning scorpion replied: 'What's logic got to do with it? It's just my character.'

We have to admit that character is a very perplexing thing. What is it that makes some people

behave in a way which is plain beastly and others
in a way which is kindness itself? Over the last
fifty years or so the arguments have raged back
and forth between those who advocate the domi-
nant influence of nature on the one hand, and those
who would stress nurture on the other. 'Heredity
or environment?' goes the cry.

Some, like Professor H. Eysenck, put most of
our character and behaviour down to what we in-
herit from our parents, with our genetic make-up
being the decisive factor. It may be that we have
some sympathy with this view, after all, those who
are parents can testify to the remarkable difference in character between children of the same
sex who otherwise have been treated more or less
the same; how like grandfather little William is
and how like Uncle Ralph, Billy has become.

Others, like Professor B. F. Skinner, stress the
environment in which people are raised as being
decisive in determining the type of character developed. Again, we may in good measure agree,
for it does seem reasonable to expect that a stimulating home environment, with parents taking an
active interest in their children's lives, will produce different results from homes in which the
children are more or less ignored or simply stuck
in front of the automated baby-sitter called the
TV.

Therefore, we may conclude that there is some

truth in both of these positions, although I would suspect that the full story is much more complex and subtle than either school of thought would admit. But whatever factors determine our character, the Bible makes it quite clear that *we* are personally responsible for the way we behave and the choices we make.

This is a truth which is underscored for us in another incident, recorded in chapter 5 of John's Gospel, the account of the remarkable healing of the man at the pool of Bethesda. Here we come face to face with two characters who are almost diametrically opposed to each other. There is the paralytic whom, as we shall see, was somewhat like the scorpion, having a very nasty sting in his tail, and there is Jesus who most certainly does take after his Father, being the perfect and complete expression of the character of God himself.

God's sovereignty and man's suffering

Some time later, Jesus went up to Jerusalem for a feast of the Jews. Now there is in Jerusalem near the Sheep Gate a pool, which in Aramaic is called Bethesda and which is surrounded by five covered colonnades. Here a great number of disabled people used to lie – the blind, the lame, the paralysed. One who was there had been an invalid for thirty-eight years. When Jesus saw him lying there and learned that he had been in this condi-

*tion for a long time, he asked him, 'Do you want
to get well?'* (5:1-6).

Here is a pool, which is purported to have powers of healing, shimmering in the sun, surrounded
by five covered colonnades. Spread over the whole
floor area are sick people, rows and rows of them,
some blind, some crippled, others with withered
limbs. And straightaway we are confronted with
what many would regard as a perplexing problem. Why out of the scores lying sick that day did
Jesus heal only one person?

After all, there were plenty of others who had
been confined to that place for years, hoping
against hope that some sort of relief might be
found for their miseries; what was so special about
this man? In fact, there was nothing special about
him at all, at least not in terms of having anything
which commended him to Jesus. Indeed, it appears that the opposite is true; he proves to be
something of a grouchy, self-centred, thankless
man whose sickness was somehow tied to his sin.
Therefore, we ask on what basis should he be sin-
gled out for special treatment?

The simple answer (and I suspect the only answer) is that that is what Jesus decided to do. It
was his free sovereign choice to do so. After all,
God is no man's debtor, he doesn't have to heal or
show mercy. If he chooses to, then he does so out
of his own free volition and for no other reason.

But, you say, that isn't fair. True, fairness has nothing to do with it. It is grace, *undeserved* mercy, that is in operation here.

This is a very important point which Christians in the West need to grasp. Contrary to the myth which is presently being generated, Jesus did not heal all those he came into contact with. To hear some people speak, what Jesus should have done on this occasion was to have held a healing meeting, but he didn't.

In fact he *never* called a healing meeting. Either he healed at a specific request of individuals or he took the initiative to heal once it was established that he was in the area for some other purpose, as in this case, where we are told that Jesus was present for a religious festival.

Does this mean, therefore, that Jesus couldn't heal all those other folk, or that something was missing in them – faith perhaps? Not at all. He could have healed but he chose not to, and lack of spiritual receptivity certainly wasn't the problem, for if it was, then this fellow shouldn't have been healed at all, for he was as dull as anyone could be.

To the question 'Can God heal?' the answer is 'Yes'. To the question 'Does God always heal?' the answer is 'No'. He is the sovereign Lord who works according to his purpose which may not be the same as ours. If we are going to spare our-

selves and many others from a lot of unnecessary
anguish in the Christian life, then it is vital that
we get that truth firmly lodged in our minds.

An offer that can't be refused

Here, then, is Jesus in what looks more like a hos-
pital than a public bath, and he asks this one man
who for thirty-eight years has been coming along
to this health spa: 'Do you want to get well?' What
a question! We may think that the answer would
be obvious. Indeed, the question has all the sensi-
tivity of a sick joke. But that would be to miss the
pastoral genius of Jesus.

In a roundabout way he is asking: 'Do you want
to get well? Then look no further'; it's an offer
he's making. However, the problem is that the paralytic wants to take up the offer, but on the wrong
terms. For a start, instead of thankful gratitude
expressed in faith, there is barbed begrudging
contempt: *'Sir ... I have no-one to help me into
the pool when the water is stirred. While I am trying to get in, someone else goes down ahead of
me'* (5:7).

He's exasperated with Jesus' question which
he considers to be a little stupid. 'Of course I want
to get well; why do you think I'm here in the first
place? But fat chance I have, for whenever the moment comes and the healing powers of the waters
are available, I get pushed out of the way.' So at

least implicitly the suggestion is that if Jesus wants to help him, then he can do so by making sure he can get into the pool at the appropriate time.

It is helpful to understand a little of the background to this event. Popular folklore held that from time to time an angel appeared in this pool, not that anyone had seen it, but there would be a rippling and movement of the waters which, according to tradition, was the action of an angelic being. It was believed that the first person into the water after it had been stirred would be healed. In other words, what we are confronted with is folk-religion – superstition. Instead of turning to Jesus, the Son of God, the giver of life for healing, the paralytic was pinning his hopes on religious mumbo jumbo.

It is tragic when credence is given to this sort of thing, as happened in the middle ages when thousands of people went on pilgrimages to Canterbury Cathedral to touch the relic of Thomas Becket to be healed, or as people do today in going to Lourdes. It's the same thing; superstitious folk-religion with a veneer of Christianity.

'But surely', it is objected, 'there is evidence of healings associated with these places?' That I don't doubt, any more than I doubt some Christian Science or Hindu testimonies to healings. The question is: what has such folk-religion got to do with the wholesome, Christ-centred faith of the

New Testament? This episode alone strongly suggests that the answer is nothing at all.

As if cutting the man dead in his tracks before he can make another unhelpful remark, Jesus issues a powerful word of command: *'Get up! Pick up your mat and walk'* (5:8). At once he is cured – a healing that is impressive by any standards. Here we see how powerful the word of Christ is. No bell, book or candle incantations here, but a pronouncement of the powerful word of God, spoken by the Son of God.

But please notice how provocative that word is too. When Jesus is at work, you can expect opposition to be just around the corner:

The day on which this took place was a Sabbath, and so the Jews said to the man who had been healed, 'It is the Sabbath, the law forbids you to carry your mat.'

But he replied, 'The man who made me well said to me, "Pick up your mat and walk."'

So they asked him, 'Who is this fellow who told you to pick it up and walk?' (5:9b-12).

Isn't that amazing? A most wonderful act of compassion has taken place, a miracle of breathtaking proportions, and what do we find? We find narrow-minded religiosity on the one hand and self-centred ingratitude on the other.

Rules, rules, rules

The religious authorities were so concerned with petty unbiblical rules and regulations that they were blinded to the glory of the Son of God and the needs of sinful man. This is religious bureaucracy gone mad.

In the Old Testament, work on the Sabbath was forbidden. But what constituted 'work'? That was a question that occupied the mind of many of the leading rabbis of the time. In the Old Testament, the answer is quite simple, it was one's normal means of employment. However, this man's job wasn't carrying mats for a living, so strictly speaking he wasn't breaking the law.

But what the Jews had done was to add to what the Old Testament taught. In fact, they drew up a list of 39 classes of work prohibited on the Sabbath – 39 rules and regulations which would have made the most ambitious civil servant blush with embarrassment!

Sadly it is only too easy to be so concerned with unbiblical matters that we lose sight of the gospel. For example, how much water do you use in baptism? More heat than light has been generated over that one. I've had it said to me that the only version of the Bible Christians should use is the Authorised Version (after all, it was good enough for the Apostle Paul!). We can all add to the list issues and concerns which simply con-

sume people's attention, taking them further away
from the things that really matter, like love.

Not even a 'thank you'

But what of the ingratitude of the man? He hadn't
even bothered to find out who it was who healed
him. When these clergymen asked him who had
told him to pick up the mat, he hadn't any idea as
to the answer. How ungrateful can one get! If a
surgeon was to save your life I would assume that
you would want to know his name so that you
could thank him. Not this man. According to verse
14 it was Jesus who found *him,* not he who looked
for Jesus: *Later Jesus found him at the temple and
said to him, 'See, you are well again. Stop sinning or something worse may happen to you.'*

But what is particularly interesting is that in
this case Jesus gave him a warning to be careful
how he lived in the future, otherwise some greater
catastrophe might befall him. In Jesus' mind at
least, there was a connection between the man's
physical infirmity and his sinful state. We are not
told what that relationship is, but the implication
is unmistakable.

Sin is powerful in its effects and we ignore that
truth at our peril. But let that be qualified by saying that not all illness is a direct result of particular sinful behaviour or attitudes, only some.

But note what he does: *The man went away*

and told the Jews that it was Jesus who had made him well (5:14). Straight away he searches out the religious authorities whom he knows want to get their hands on whoever it was who, in their opinion, was wantonly promoting irreligious behaviour (carrying a mat on a Sabbath) and tells them that the man they are looking for is none other than Jesus.

What made him do such a thing? Maybe it was Jesus saying to him, 'Stop sinning or something worse may happen to you.' Perhaps that was what raised his hackles: 'Who does Jesus think he is, telling me I'm a sinner. I'm a victim requiring understanding and sympathy, not a criminal deserving judgment and a warning. I'll soon put him in his place.' So off he goes.

And of course, in so doing he does precisely what Jesus warns him not to do; he sins. We may ask, 'Is it possible for those who have received such blessings from Jesus, such kindness, then to turn their back on him and so betray him?' Sadly, yes, it is only too possible.

Christianity without commitment
It is a sad fact of life that there are many who wish to receive the blessings of Christ without wanting commitment to Christ; those who wish to receive his forgiveness but not his correction.

An example which the writer Don Carson gives

makes the point only too well. [1] He speaks of a
man, a medical doctor and former missionary, who
was appointed as one of the leaders in a church,
an elder. Some time later he had an affair, divorced
his wife, abandoned his children, and separated
himself off from any form of biblical Christianity. Countless attempts were made to rehabilitate
him, and they all failed.

But, says Carson, the most thoughtful assessment of the mess came from one of the leaders in
the church. He suggested that the doctor, who
came from a Christian home and had done all the
'right' things, had never had to make a decision
that cost him anything. Even his missionary work
was bound up with his own speciality interest in
medicine. Everything was too easy.

But then troubles began to open up his marriage (as they do in every marriage at one time or
another), and when an attractive alternative presented herself, this doctor had no real moral centre on which to depend. He had never for the sake
of Christ taken a decision which cost him something, and he wasn't going to start now.

So it is, here. Incur the wrath of the religious
authorities? No, far better to ingratiate oneself
with them than engage in a costly following of
Jesus. Sure, take Jesus' words of blessing, but not

---

1. *How Long, O Lord!*, D A Carson, IVP, 1990.

his words of rebuke. Better to hedge your bets with the world than get too carried away with a Christian faith that might actually cost you something. That was this man's position and it is not unique.

This story stands as a solemn warning to us all. Christ is willing by the gospel message to impart real spiritual healing, the healing of the spiritual paralysis in our lives caused by our sin. But we are not to think that this gives us a free licence to live as we want, making his forgiveness cheap. There is nothing cheap about the cross where he suffered and paid the price for our misdoings. No, he wants followers who are ready and willing, whatever the cost, to follow him and go his way. The question is: are we willing?

7

Jesus meets a blind man
(John 9:1-41)

Is fire a good thing or a bad thing? I guess the answer all depends upon what it is used for and its effect. Fire is good in that it can keep us warm when otherwise we would freeze. It is good in that it enables us to prepare food which otherwise would remain inedible. But then again, it is a bad thing in that it can kill or reduce precious woodland to a smouldering stubble.

What about light, is that a good thing or a bad thing? Again it depends upon its effect. Without light we can't see where we are going or appreciate the beautiful things around us. But that same light which is so precious can also be very damaging, as when an intensely bright flash from an explosion blinds.

In the passage that we are looking at in this chapter, we hear Jesus reiterating a truth about himself which points to him having two effects in the world: namely, enlightening those who are spiritually blind and are willing to admit it, and blinding those who are determined to persist in their unbelief.

The saying which captures these twin truths is found in verse 5 when Jesus proclaims: *'I am the light of the world.'* Not 'a light', one light amongst many, but *the* light. Immediately we are faced with the truth that when people are confronted with Jesus there is no neutrality – either you are for him or you are against him; you either receive his healing touch or you repudiate it. But whatever you do, you cannot ignore him.

In one of the most dramatic stories in the Gospels, this startling truth is brought home to us with breathtaking force – the story of the healing of the man born blind.

A problem faced

As he went along, he saw a man blind from birth. His disciples asked him, 'Rabbi, who sinned, this man or his parents, that he was born blind?'

'Neither this man nor his parents sinned,' said Jesus, 'but this happened so that the work of God might be displayed in his life. As long as it is day, we must do the work of him who sent me. Night is coming, when no-one can work. While I am in the world, I am the light of the world!' (9:1-4).

Jesus and his disciples were walking along the road when they came across this poor man who was something of a local celebrity by virtue of

the tragic fact that he had been blind from birth.
And we can be sure that many a discussion had
centred upon this fellow, with people trying to discover some sort of explanation for his state. It is
the question we still hear asked today: 'Why does
God allow innocent suffering?'

It is interesting that whereas the disciples see
this as an occasion for a misguided theological
discussion: 'Who sinned, this man or his parents?',
with the implication, 'It must be God's judgment',
Jesus, however, takes it as an opportunity to dem-
onstrate God's redeeming power: 'Neither, but this
happened *so that* the work of God might be displayed in his life.'

What we are given here is a valuable insight
into one of the ways we should approach the whole
question of suffering. The traditional approach is
to look back for a reason, asking the questions:
What is the cause of suffering? Who sinned?
Where did it all come from in the first place? But
Jesus changes the focus so that we ask not, 'What
is the cause?', but 'What is the purpose? What
possible good can come out of suffering?'

In the healing that follows, not only is there an
immediate physical benefit for the man, but more
importantly, there is a spiritual benefit as he comes
to know the Saviour. In fact, his healing becomes
a sign of what Jesus can do spiritually for anyone
who comes to him – he gives them sight so that

they can come to know God personally.

Is it not often the case that in and through suffering God does display his work? Not always in physical healing, but in leading us to a deeper knowledge of himself.

One Christian woman who testifies to this truth is Mary Craig, who describes how two of her four sons were born with severe abnormalities, one with Hohler's syndrome and the other with Down's syndrome. In her account she speaks of redemptive suffering and so writes:

> In the teeth of the evidence I do not believe that any suffering is ultimately pointless or absurd, although it is often difficult to go on convincing oneself of this. At first we react with incredulity, anger and despair. Yet the value of suffering does not lie in the pain of it but in what the sufferer makes of it. It is in sorrow that we discover ourselves.[1]

That is precisely the perspective that Jesus introduces here: God displaying his work in the most unpromising of situations.

Jesus begins to perform the miracle by gently rubbing a mud poultice on the man's eyes and sending him away to wash in the pool of Siloam,

---

1. *Blessings*, Mary Craig, Hodder and Stoughton, 1979.

with the amazing result that the man goes home seeing for the very first time in his life. And no sooner are his eyes getting used to the daylight, than the poor fellow finds himself at the centre of a major controversy.

His neighbours and those who had formerly seen him begging asked, 'Isn't this the same man who used to sit and beg?' Some claimed that he was.

Others said, 'No, he only looks like him.'

But he himself insisted, 'I am the man' (9:8).

Some staring at him began to wonder if it were they who needed their eyes tested! They must have made a mistake, it must be someone else, why, it can't be the man who was *born* blind. Others fighting back their incredulity admitted that he was the same man and naturally they wanted to know the explanation: who was responsible?

Have you noticed that whenever something spectacular happens in the world, the media wheel in an expert for comment? If there is an economic collapse, in comes the financial man from the city. If there is some scientific discovery, there is the boffin from the university. And if there is some religious news, then it is usually some unbelieving clergyman who is called upon to deny it if it is orthodox.

Things were not so different in Jesus' day. Here was News with a capital N, and if the reason why

the man was born blind raised one or two theological questions, his healing raised even more,
and so the Pharisees were approached for their
opinion: *They brought to the Pharisees the man
who had been blind* (9:13).

A prejudice encountered

To say that from the outset the Pharisees had a
king-sized prejudice against Jesus would be something of an understatement. It was a prejudice centred on that little incidental detail which John
records for us in verse 14: *Now the day on which
Jesus had made the mud and opened the man's
eyes was a Sabbath.*

According to the traditions that had been added
to what the Old Testament taught about the Sabbath, Jesus was found guilty of breaking those traditions on no fewer than three counts. First he
made a mud poultice, and that was considered to
be work. Second, he anointed the eyes, which also
constituted work, and thirdly he healed, which too,
in the opinion of the Pharisees, was work. The
conclusion was inescapable, Jesus was a sinner
and God doesn't work through lawbreakers like
him: *Some of the Pharisees said, 'This man is not
from God, for he does not keep the Sabbath'*
(9:16).

Even if it is a proper miracle, that in itself
proves nothing. According to these 'experts', the

man cannot be from God – *a priori*. But then there are others who in the latter part of verse 16 say, 'Look, the miracle is so astounding, how can we believe that Jesus is such a scoundrel? Surely only God can perform a miracle of such magnitude?' The question raised is: which group was right? In fact they were both right and both wrong.

The first group was at least right in their *approach* to the question in so far as they tried to make an assessment based upon Scripture. They took what the Old Testament said about the sanctity of the Sabbath seriously, reasoning that anyone who flagrantly disregarded God's law was a rebel, a sinner, and so even if he were a miracle-worker the miracles could not have come from God. But of course where they went wrong was in their *interpretation* of Scripture, distorting what it actually taught about the Sabbath, and therefore they were bound to be wrong in their conclusion.

The other group, however, was right in their *conclusion*, correctly doubting that Jesus was sinful, but wrong in their method. They were starting from experience and saying that the miracle in and of itself must prove that it is of God. They were arguing from the results. But of course that proves nothing of the sort.

The Old Testament, and indeed the New Testament, is full of warnings that false prophets will be able to perform miracles (e.g. Deuteronomy

13:1-5; Mark 13:22). Today there are sects and cults who have the most impressive track record of the good effects they have produced in people's lives: reducing stress, making people feel happy and so on. Even some Muslims exhibit the phenomena of speaking in tongues and prophecy. So are we legitimately to conclude that God is at work in all of these things? Of course not.

Therefore, both groups were prejudiced against Jesus in that they had a faulty understanding of who he is. One group saw him as a blasphemer and so this alleged miracle must have some other explanation. The second group saw him as little more than a miracle-worker and not as the one who deserved allegiance and worship as the Son of God.

The tragedy is that their prejudices were so strong that they tried to find some alternative explanation. Accordingly, they turned to the man himself and asked his opinion with the hope that maybe he would come down on their side: *What have you to say about him? It was your eyes he opened* (9:17). And you almost detect the unbelieving tone in the way that question was put.

It is ironic that here was a man who probably had never had a day's schooling in his life, who felt out of his depth in the midst of such august company and who was yet much nearer the truth than they would ever be: *He is a prophet,* he says, meaning a man from God. He knew what God had done in his life and that it tied in with Scripture and that was enough for him.

Yet in spite of the man's own testimony, and in spite of what other people had obviously said, they still did not believe that he had been blind, but that somehow it was all a confidence trick. Still dissatisfied, they dragged in the parents who were faced with a dilemma. They couldn't deny that he was their son, nor could they deny that he had been blind, what is more they couldn't deny that he could now see. But they were not going to attempt to provide an explanation of what happened, for that was more than their life was worth.

'How he can see now, or who opened his eyes, we don't know. Ask him. He is of age; he will speak for himself.' His parents said this because they were afraid of the Jews, for already the Jews had decided that anyone who acknowledged that Jesus was the Christ would be put out of the synagogue (9:21).

This line of enquiry was obviously proving to be a dead end, so what else could be the explanation? The answer was obvious, the blind man must be hiding something: *A second time they summoned the man who had been blind. 'Give glory to God,' they said. 'We know this man is a sinner'* (9:24). What this means is not 'Praise God for what he has done – give him the glory and not

Jesus', but rather, 'Before God own up and tell us
the truth; on oath confirm our belief that Jesus is
a sinner.' Do you see how prejudice blinds people
from the truth? It's the old old story of 'Don't
confuse me with the facts, my mind is made up.'

Sadly the same is true today. The Bible clearly
spells out that Jesus is no ordinary man, he is the
Son of God who came to rescue people, giving
them eternal life. Why is it that in spite of the overwhelming evidence of the Bible, even as history,
that people still refuse to take Jesus seriously? For
precisely the same reasons as we have here.

In the first place, many people have preconceived ideas about Jesus and Christianity. It is my
experience as I talk to people about the Christian
faith, that Jesus is seen as being just a good religious leader but not as being of crucial significance to us today. This is nothing but a preconceived picture which is way out of line with what
the biblical data presents us with. 'Yes, we will
have him as a good man, an inspiration to us all,
but not as the one who deserves total allegiance
as Lord and God.'

However, as C. S. Lewis once observed, Christianity and its claims about Christ is either of such
vital importance that our whole lives depend upon
it, or it is of no importance whatsoever and therefore can be ignored. But we can never be allowed
to go away thinking that it is only of moderate

importance. It is either all or nothing; a view with which the apostle John would have wholeheartedly agreed.

In the second place, people are prevented from seeing the truth because they have cherished beliefs which they simply won't let go of. Why is it that for the last century and a half there has been a sustained attack by theologians and church leaders on the divinity of Christ?

One reason is because if Christ is truly divine and unique, it relativizes all other religions and scotches every attempt to bring all the different faiths together. And the fact is some people are so committed to the idea that all roads lead to God, or that everyone will get to heaven in the end, that they have to cut out bits from the Bible which do not fit in with that 'one world dream'.

But by far the most common reason why people do not take the claims of Jesus seriously is because they know that it will be too challenging and they will have to change. As G. K. Chesterton once said, 'It is not that Christianity has been tried and found wanting. It is that it has been found demanding and therefore not tried.'

It is simply too challenging, and like the blind man's parents many of us are afraid of the cost that the truth might bring with it. Or like the Pharisees we would have to alter radically our way of thinking and behaving if we accepted that Jesus

is to be number one in our lives, and that is just
too threatening to contemplate.

Therefore, we have to find some reason for explaining away the evidence, or hide behind a bar-
rage of questions in the hope that they will divert
attention: 'What about creation and evolution?'
'What about suffering?' 'What about all the con-
tradictions in the Bible?' When really the bottom
line is fear of facing up to the truth and the change
that will entail.

But the one who has encountered Christ
through the gospel *must* speak the truth and face
the consequences.

*Then they hurled insults at him and said: 'You
are this fellow's disciple! We are disciples of Moses! We know that God spoke to Moses, but as for
this fellow, we don't even know where he comes
from.'*

*The man answered, 'Now that is remarkable!
You don't know where he comes from, yet he
opened my eyes. We know that God does not listen to sinners. He listens to the godly man who
does his will. Nobody has ever heard of opening
the eyes of a man born blind. If this man were not
from God, he could do nothing.'*

*To this they replied, 'You were steeped in sin at
birth; how dare you lecture us!' And they threw
him out* (9:28-34).

The believer has Scripture, reason and experience on his side, but it can be all too much for some people, so they react with violence.

Let me ask: How do you react when you hear someone speaking about Christ, telling of what he has done? Do you rejoice in it? Do you welcome it, even if it challenges you and shows up inadequacies in your life? Or does it grate on you, make you feel uncomfortable and so you try to dismiss it as religious enthusiasm? Depending upon the answer you give to those questions, you can assess where you stand in relation to the Christian faith. Whether you are in fact on the inside so that you can say with the man, 'Once I was blind but now I see', or whether you stand with the Pharisees on the outside.

The primary purpose

What is the purpose of Jesus coming into the world? *Jesus said, 'For judgment I have come into this world, so that the blind will see and those who see will become blind'* (9:39). What does Jesus mean? He means at least this; that those who are honest enough, humble enough and open enough to recognize that they are spiritually blind, Christ will give them sight. This man is like that; he admits in verses 25 and 32 how little he knows, except that he was blind. It is to such people that Jesus becomes the light of life, so that they have a perception, a personal knowledge of God through

his Son which is second to none. But we also have
the warning to those who claim that they can see,
claiming that they know for sure who Jesus is,
and yet are profoundly wrong.

*Some Pharisees who were with him heard him
say this and asked, 'What? Are we blind too?'*

*Jesus said, 'If you were blind, you would not
be guilty of sin; but now that you claim you can
see, your guilt remains'* (9:40-41).

They will simply be condemned in their unbelief. Do you see the seriousness of resisting God's
revelation, refusing to consider it and be chal-
lenged by it? For if you are in this position then
you are on the sure way to eternal blindness, in-
habiting the place Jesus refers to as outer darkness. I can think of nothing more tragic and more
frightening than seeing people on the last day who
have had the Christian message explained to them,
and yet have rejected it by clinging to some inferior explanation, only to discover themselves
struck blind and forever confirmed in the state
they have persisted in (Revelation 22:11).

However, the greatest joy that can ever be
known is to have our eyes opened spiritually so
that we can understand and know who Jesus is
and follow him in love and obedience for the rest
of our lives. No doubt with this incident in mind
the one-time slave-trader John Newton captured
his experience well in his famous hymn:

Amazing grace! how sweet the sound,
   That saved a wretch like me!
I once was lost, but now am found;
   Was blind, but now I see.

8

Jesus meets a devoted follower
(John 12:1-8)

As we look around at the state of the church in the West today, what would we say is its most urgent need?

Some would say it is the need for *greater purity in the area of sexual matters*. In a recent survey conducted by Morton Hunt, he demonstrated what he calls the complete eroticization of our culture over the last three decades. The importance that people attribute to achieving complete sexual fulfilment has reached an unprecedented level. And all the signs are that in spite of the devastating impact that AIDS is going to have on our culture, sexual promiscuity shows no signs of abating.

Therefore, it comes as no surprise that, as society in general has been mastered by the so-called sexual revolution, the Christian society has also been captured, at least in part. In a recent survey amongst evangelical young-people's groups in this country, it was revealed that 45 per cent of the twenty-year-olds who were single had had intercourse at some time in their life. Admittedly, this would have included some sexual experience before becoming Christians, but a good proportion was after becoming believers. So it looks like the modern adage 'If it feels good do it' has infected Christian thinking at the most fundamental level.

Others would point to the *incessant craving of consumerism* as that which requires our greatest attention. The new temples devoted to the god mammon are the superstores and DIY centres vying successfully for idolatrous devotion, even on a Sunday. Like a junky requiring his next fix, the feverish desire for more and more screams at a person as the only way of filling that aching inner void.

But can the modern Christian claim that this is not part of his or her experience too? An earlier generation of believers with their treasures stored firmly in heaven would have taken a simple attitude to these matters: if we can't afford it, we don't have it. More to the point, if it was a choice between us going without and God's work being neglected, it was a foregone conclusion which came first. How things have changed!

But with only 5 per cent of the population worshipping in church in Britain each Sunday, some would point to *evangelism* as the priority for the church.

We may consider these and a dozen other concerns which we feel are the needs of the moment, and no doubt in some measure many would be right. But I want to suggest that our greatest need is nothing less than *a costly, self-effacing devotion to Christ.*

And this simple but much needed truth is brought out for us in John 12. What we are presented with here is a sharply focused contrast between Mary on the one hand and Judas on the other; between an unbelievably extravagant gesture flowing from a heart full of love, and pious words masking a heart full of hate.

A special occasion

Six days before the Passover, Jesus arrived at Bethany, where Lazarus lived, whom Jesus had raised from the dead. Here a dinner was given in Jesus' honour. Martha served, while Lazarus was among those reclining at the table with him. Then Mary took about a pint of pure nard, an expensive perfume; she poured it on Jesus' feet and wiped his feet with her hair. And the house was filled with the fragrance of the perfume (12:1-3).

Here is a small town just outside Jerusalem, Bethany, which had been shaken by one of the greatest events ever known; the raising of a man who had been lying in the grave for four days. Lazarus was a walking miracle. People would stare at him in the street, mothers would point him out to their children and whisper, 'That's him.' And no doubt if television had been around at the time he would have been a popular chat-show guest!

But what was really causing a stir and getting people excited was the news that the one who had performed the miracle, Jesus, was in town. A man like that you don't let go of easily. You want to find out more about him, and so the town dignitaries and several important families had a special banquet arranged with Jesus as guest of honour.

True devotion

As they sat around the low table, enjoying the meal, no doubt having a stimulating conversation, suddenly one of the women did something which would have brought the whole proceedings to a grinding halt.

Mary, the sister of Lazarus, carefully produced a delicate alabaster jar containing pure nard, an incredibly sweet and immensely expensive perfume originating from India. It may have been a family heirloom, we don't know, but what we do know is that if you worked six days a week for a whole year, bought no food, paid no rent, bought no clothes, but saved all the money you had earned, you would just about scrape together enough to buy a pint of this stuff. Which is precisely what Mary had done.

And what did she do with it? She poured it

over Jesus' feet. No-one forced her to do it, she did it willingly. And why? Because in some tangible way, in a way which goes beyond mere words, she wanted to express her love and appreciation for her Lord.

As far as she was concerned nothing could be too much. Mary was devoted to Christ, she hung on every word that he uttered, she knew he was someone special, one sent from God. She could never forget that it was this Jesus who had raised her brother from the dead and mended her broken heart. And so in an act of pure extravagance, she showed her devotion to Christ.

As we look around ourselves in the church in the West today, where do we find that sort of costly devotion? We find it in the Christian couple who say, 'We may not have had our brother raised from the dead, but the Lord Jesus has raised us spiritually from the dead and we are thankful. Therefore when we see a need in the church fellowship we are determined to help meet that need at whatever personal cost to ourselves.' I know of one family which sold their house and moved into a smaller one so that the money raised could be used for Christ's work. Does that shock us? If it does, then it is perhaps that we have far more in common with Judas than with Mary.

But this was not only to cost Mary financially, it was to cost her dignity, for we read in verse 3:

She wiped Jesus' feet with her hair. This act may
seem strange to us, but it was absolutely scandal-
ous to these people, for in that culture it was a
shameful thing for a woman to let her hair down
in public. But then to go further and wipe a man's
feet with it was bordering on the obscene.

Have you ever been in a situation where someone says or does something which leaves everyone in stunned embarrassment and you just don't
know where to put yourself? That was the situation
here. But social convention or no social convention, Mary was so determined to show her loyalty
and love to Jesus that she didn't care at all about
what other people thought or what they might have
said about her behind her back – how loose she
was, how socially inferior she was – all that mat-
tered was her selfless commitment to Christ.

Is it not the case that we are so often held back
in giving ourselves over to Christ because we are
bothered about what others may think of us? 'Oh
Bill, you know, he's alright, but he does take this
Christianity lark a little *too* seriously'; 'Joan, nice
woman, but you won't believe this, the other day
in the office I actually caught her praying – very
odd'; 'And Johnny, great rugby player, don't get
me wrong, but you will never guess what he does
at the weekend – he teaches in a Sunday school!'
Although such comments might be irksome, they
do not even begin to match up to the price some

Christians have to pay for their devotion to Christ.

The chaplain of the University of New South Wales in Australia at the 1993 Evangelical Ministry Assembly went on record saying that in some of the ethnic groups around the campus, active opposition is experienced by those who become Christians from those groups.

For example, one young Korean committed his life to Christ, and as he was driving to church one morning his own father put a brick through the car window and nearly killed him. The father said that if he persisted in going to church then every time he came home he would find his mother beaten. Being a violent man he was as good as his word and it happened.

One Greek girl who became a Christian found herself in the situation where every time she came back from church her two brothers would beat her.

One Lebanese student, during the first six months of becoming a Christian, was placed under virtual house-arrest by her parents. They took her away from the university and locked her in the house. That is costly devotion.

To a certain extent there is a link between the degree of devotion to Jesus Christ and the degree of opposition experienced. Without wishing to foster a martyr mentality, it is largely true to say that if we are serious about our Christian faith, then we can expect difficulty. And if we are not experiencing criticism, then perhaps we ought to take another look at our discipleship to see how genuine it really is.

False concern

However, it is when the criticism comes from those whom we thought were on our side, other 'Christians', that it stings the most:

But one of the disciples, Judas Iscariot, who was later to betray him, objected, 'Why wasn't this perfume sold and the money given to the poor? It was worth a year's wages.' He did not say this because he cared about the poor but because he was a thief; as keeper of the money bag, he used to help himself to what was put into it (12:4-6).

This was not only the feeling of Judas, it was a view shared by all the other disciples as Mark tells us in his account of the same incident (Mark 14:4). We can be sure that if we show true love for the Lord, then criticism will come. But it sounds so reasonable, so religious: 'What a waste! Think of how many starving stomachs could have been fed had this woman done the decent thing and sold the perfume to raise some money for Live Aid.' But Judas' real motive was quite different, he wanted the money for himself. Pious words coming from one of Jesus' right-hand men, the church treasurer no less, and yet it was all a sham.

It is sad to say that there is a tendency when

someone acts in a way that is challenging to us, for us to demean it and even use high-sounding ethical arguments to ensure that we are immunized from its challenge.

I have been in churches where some enterprise expressing devotion to Christ has been embarked upon, maybe a building project, or sending Bibles to Eastern Europe, or supporting a Christian worker abroad, and the objections have come in thick and fast: 'What a waste of money. What about the poor, the unemployed, what about thinking of our own country first rather than those foreigners?' Yes, even members of churches can say such things.

But when one replies, 'Fair enough, that's your decision, you may not want to give money to this project or that cause, but how much are you giving to the poor or unemployed which you seem so concerned about?', then the silence is deafening. What is more, when you look at the homes of such Christians you can see where most of their money is going. If we are not careful we can end up being a thief and robbing God, just as surely as if our name were Judas.

Right priorities
However, Jesus does not respond by saying, 'Of course, foolish young girl, when you grow up you will be much more measured and wise in your

use of things – it's youthful religious enthusiasm, you know.' Not at all, it is the disciples who receive the rebuke: *'Leave her alone,' Jesus replied. 'It was meant that she should save this perfume for the day of my burial'* (12:7).

In other words, Jesus is saying that Mary has got her priorities right and she has done far more in this act of costly devotion than even she realizes. For this anointing with perfume, which was traditionally done to one who had died, points to Jesus' own death on the cross.

'*You will always have the poor among you, but you will not always have me,*' says Jesus (12:8). In recent years there has been an ongoing debate within the church over the relationship between evangelism and social action, centring on the question of which is to have priority. Some have said that there is no real conflict but the two should go together, telling people the gospel and helping in their need.

In practice that might be so, but ultimately, in terms of priority and principle, that can't be correct, for telling people about how they can be put right with God and receive eternal life must take precedence, if we are going to be true to the Bible. Rightly we are moved by the sight of starving children on our TV screens, rightly we should be moved to take compassionate action to alleviate such suffering. Here lies the advantage of the camera.

But what if we could film a soul going to hell? What if we could capture the appalling misery of someone spending an eternity in utter agony, crying out without Christ? Maybe then we would understand why Jesus says what he says, why he did not give himself over to a lifetime of healing the sick and feeding the poor, but instead chose to die in pain-wrenching agony on a cross for people like us, to spare us from the ghastly horrors of hell. And perhaps if we could see such pictures, that is, see as God sees, then we might not be so complacent in our evangelism and prayer life as we tend to be. The priority is surrendering our life to Christ and telling others that they must surrender their lives to him too.

But it doesn't end there, because when Jesus said 'the poor you will always have with you', he is in fact quoting Deuteronomy 15:11 which goes on to say, 'Therefore I command you to be openhanded towards your brothers and towards the poor and needy in your land.' It is taken as read by Jesus that his followers will know that scripture and obey it to the full. If we love Christ we will love the needy and give, but we have to get the order right.

So the question facing us is this: where do we stand in practice? Are we with Mary, devoted to Christ, loving him, showing that love in costly self-giving, regardless of what others might think or say? Or are we in fact with Judas; apparently re-spectable, apparently 'Christian', but yet never having submitted to Christ's rule in our hearts? It's all a sham.

What is the church's greatest need? It is a costly, self-effacing devotion to Christ.

9

Jesus meets despondent followers
(John 14:1-14)

There are few things which are more unsettling to the human mind than uncertainty about the future. This is especially so if the signs are that the future carries prospects of turbulence and difficulty. Of course, all of this is understandable. In many ways we are creatures of habit, valuing the routine which gives us a sense of security. That is why we tend to react with disbelief, if not outright hostility, when it is suggested that far from the future being routine and predictable it is going to be disrupted and unruly. Worse still, if the spectre of death lurks ominously on the horizon.

Such a chill in the pit of the stomach was precisely what Jesus' disciples were experiencing on that fateful night when Jesus took them to one side to explain to them that things would never be the same. They were thinking that they were on the verge of some major political and religious breakthrough. As far as they were concerned they had hitched their wagon to a star – Jesus – quite certain that nothing could stop them.

Then suddenly Jesus started to talk about betrayal, arrests, torture and death. Little wonder
that their blood turned to ice and the veins in the
side of their heads began to pulsate with bewil-
dered anxiety. What on earth could he be talking
about? Here is the man who fed 5,000 people, who
turned water into wine, who healed the man born
blind and raised the dead – why such appalling
pessimism? Is he suffering from some sort of
depression, as prominent leaders are prone to do?

Those would have been some of the thoughts
which Jesus would have picked up and which lay
behind the concern addressed in verses 1-5: *'Do
not let your hearts be troubled. Trust in God; trust
also in me. In my Father's house are many rooms;
if it were not so, I would have told you. I am going
there to prepare a place for you. And if I go and
prepare a place for you I will come back and take
you to be with me that you also may be where I am.
You know the way to the place where I am going.'*

The concern of the disciples

The only house of God that the disciples would
have expected Jesus to be going to would have
been the Temple. The only palace with five-star
rooms they were wanting belonged to Caesar. In
short, their eyes were fixed on the setting up of the
kingdom of God on earth, and who better to do that
than Jesus? Therefore, far from allaying any anxi-

ety that they might have had, Jesus' puzzling talk about going away, preparing a place and coming back for them simply added fuel to the fire. And it was Thomas who said so. *Thomas said to him, 'Lord, we don't know where you are going, so how can we know the way?'* (14:5).

Good old Thomas. 'Doubting Thomas' we call him, always being perceived to be a pessimist. However, I am not so sure that such a view squares with the picture we are given of him in the Bible. In fact, on a straightforward reading he comes over as a man who is quite courageous in saying what he thinks, someone who is refreshingly honest without being a cynic. There was no air of super-spirituality about him, pretending he understood when he didn't in order to save embarrassment. He could have put on a pious look to mask his ignorance and said, 'Quite so Jesus, "the way", yes I like the sound of that. Fancy the others not knowing what you mean.'

But he didn't. He was in a mental fix and he was not ashamed to admit it. The point is, neither should we. God, as we saw with Nathanael, always respects honesty. The honest seeker God promises to meet – always. The one who says in all humility, 'Lord, I don't understand, please help me', is the one who will find help. That is precisely what happened here. Instead of Jesus rebuking Thomas, he revealed something to him.

The claim of Jesus

'I am the way and the truth and the life. No-one comes to the Father except through me' (14:6).

Did reading those words take your breath away? I doubt it. For those words are so familiar that their earth-shattering significance has become all but lost on us.

But if you were to take this verse and read it out in one of the acts of inter-faith worship that has been held in Westminster Abbey, or were to draw attention to it at an Assembly of the World Council of Churches, then I can guarantee that the reaction would be altogether different. In fact, I would go so far as to predict that the response would be one of outrage as if a blasphemy had been uttered. If you want a sure way of failing entry into the ordained ministry in some denominations today, then all you have to say is that you believe those words absolutely.

What Jesus is claiming here is both extreme and exclusive. It is extreme in that it is way out of line with popular thinking, both in his own time and now. To the Roman way of thinking at the time of Jesus, you could worship as few or as many gods as you liked. It really was a matter of 'pick and mix' in religion. Therefore, any claim that only one religion is right, or that there is only one way to God would immediately have caused bewilderment, if not outright hostility.

Furthermore, what Jesus is saying here would have given offence to any God-fearing Jew. Every Jew was brought up with the idea that God was wholly different to us, transcendent, beyond us, to be approached only through the various rituals and regulations he himself had laid down in the law of Moses. As for Jesus' claim that he as a *person* was the way to God, this would have appeared the height of arrogance, if not blasphemy. Jesus' claim is extreme.

What is more it is exclusive. It is quite impossible to get round the second part of verse 6: '*No-one comes to the Father except through me.*' It is plain and unequivocal.

Throughout John's Gospel the same exclusive claim appears time and time again in different forms. Jesus is said to be *the* light of the world, not a light (9:5). He is *the* good shepherd, not a good shepherd (10:11). He is *the* resurrection and the life, not a resurrection (11:25). Jesus claims for himself a status and standing which he will not and cannot share with anyone else – equality with God.

In so doing, he puts all other religions in their place by relativizing them. That is why there have been several rows in the Church of England recently about services which are designed to enable Christians, Muslims, Hindus and Buddhists to come together in an act of worship, for Jesus does not receive even a mention, except right at the end in some form of blessing. Such practice simply denies John 14:6.

But what does Jesus mean by saying he is the way, the truth and the life?

He is not saying that he leads the way to God, rather like an usherette might lead you to your seat in the cinema with the aid of a torch. He says, 'I am *the* way' to God, to heaven, to the place where God and man are to dwell in all eternity. That is the whole point of verse 2 about the house with many rooms. How, then, can he be the way?

He is the way to God, precisely because he is the truth and the life. Let me explain.

Jesus says that he is the truth of God, that is, the complete and perfect revelation of God. God is not some energy force of the kind we find in Star Wars or the New Age movement, he is personal. Therefore, what better way to reveal himself than in a manner that we can understand and comprehend, by becoming a person – which he did in Jesus.

How do we know that God is love? Because we see his love displayed in Jesus. How do we know that God is all powerful? Because we see his power at work in Jesus. How can we be sure that God hates sin and all that corrupts and spoils human relationships? For the simple reason that we see God hating it and dealing with it in Jesus. God's character and God's purposes are perfectly expressed in Jesus – and it is to him we are to look if we are to find God.

Jesus is also the life of God, that is, the one who mediates the dynamic, vibrant new spiritual life which God so freely gives. He is the one who imparts the living relationship with God we so desperately need, giving not endless life, which sounds rather dull and tedious, but eternal life; life in its fullness, life as it was meant to be, whereby we surrender to Jesus as Lord and enjoy his loving rule in our lives. That is something which begins now in this life and goes on to be consummated in the next.

It is because Jesus brings to us the truth about God and imparts to us the life of God that he is the way to God. When we know God as he really is, realize what he has done for us in his Son, and surrender our lives to him, only then have we 'arrived'. We *know* God, as Jesus says three chapters later: 'Now this is eternal life: that they may know you, the only true God, and Jesus Christ, whom you have sent' (John 17:3). That is what it means to be a Christian. Not simply knowing *about* God, but personally *knowing* God through his Son.

Christianity is a person-centred religion. This is another point of contrast with many of the other world religions. Other religious leaders tend to point away from themselves and say this is the way, or that is the truth, or this is the life. It is only

Jesus who says, 'I am the way, I am the truth, I am the life.'

C. S. Lewis, in his own inimitable way puts it like this: 'If you had gone to Buddha and asked, "Are you the son of Bramah?" he would have said, "My son, you are still in the vale of illusion." If you had gone to Socrates and asked, "Are you Zeus?" he would have laughed at you. If you had gone to Mohammed and asked, "Are you Allah?", he would first have rent his clothes and then cut off your head. The only person who can say that sort of thing is either God or a complete lunatic.' [1]

That is what this claim amounts to: either Jesus is who he claimed to be – God – or he is mad, or worse, he is bad, trying to deceive us. We cannot have it any other way.

No doubt this was strong medicine that Jesus was giving out and it was proving very difficult to swallow, hence Philip's reaction: *'Lord, show us the Father and that will be enough for us'* (14:8).

Perhaps Philip had in mind that extraordinary occasion recorded in the book of Exodus when Moses asked to see the glory of the Lord, but even then he was permitted to see only the aftermath as it were, the tail-end of God's glory and not God directly (Exodus 33:18-23).

---

1. 'What are we to make of Jesus Christ?'in *God In The Dock*, C. S. Lewis, Fount, 1989.

At this point Jesus would have been quite justified in turning round to Philip and saying, 'Don't be ridiculous. You should know by now that you cannot see God directly. For one thing, he is invisible; for another, if you were to see him in his naked holiness it would destroy you, sinful creature that you are.'

But Jesus doesn't say that. There is a deep, weary sigh as he answers: *'Don't you know me, Philip, even after I have been among you such a long time? Anyone who has seen me has seen the Father. How can you say, "Show us the Father"? Don't you believe that I am in the Father, and that the Father is in me?'* (14:9-10).

It is as if Jesus is saying, 'Philip, are you so blind? Has the penny not yet dropped? After all this time, have you not seen through my humanity to the divinity it embodies? It is I – I am God. I am the one who met Moses in the burning bush (Exodus 3:4). I am the one who stood with Joshua as the warrior of the Lord (Joshua 5:13-14). I am the one whose majestic robe Isaiah glimpsed as he went into the temple (Isaiah 6). I am the one whom Ezekiel encountered when he fell down as dead (Ezekiel 1:28). I am the one whom Daniel saw as the heavenly son of man (Daniel 7:13). What more proof do you want of my identity? Surely you can see that?

'At least', says Jesus, 'believe on the evidence

of the miracles I performed – miracles shot through with significance and meaning, all pointing conclusively in one direction – that I am God' (14:11).

Who is the one who through the natural process turns the water from the earth to the fruit of the vine? Jesus did it in record time, short-circuiting the natural process at the wedding in Cana (John 2). Who is the one who has power to bestow the gift of sight and give life to the dead? Jesus did it not once but several times. Who is the one who gives our daily bread? Jesus was able to do this for 5,000 people in one sitting. Surely there is only one who can do such things, expressing his character of love and concern, and it is God. 'He who has seen me *has* seen the Father.'

Philip, like so many people today, was looking for some unmediated experience of God to sweep away his doubts – maybe a vision or a tingle down the spine. 'If God is there,' people cry, 'then let him show himself to me. Let him do something spectacular.' The plain fact is, he has done something very spectacular; he has broken into the world in the form of this person, and all that is necessary is to look to this person – Jesus – who in and through his character, words and works reveals God perfectly.

Where do we discover Jesus today but in the Bible? That is where we read about him. That is where we hear him speak, and as we do so we discover a miracle taking place: no longer is Jesus a distant character in a story, a historical figure dead and gone, he becomes the living Lord, dwelling in our lives by his Spirit, and the consequences of this truth are really quite beyond belief.

'I tell you the truth, anyone who has faith in me will do what I have been doing. He will do even greater things than these, because I am going to the Father. And I will do whatever you ask in my name, so that the Son may bring glory to the Father. You may ask me for anything in my name, and I will do it' (14:12-14).

This verse is often taken as a proof text by those who think that Christians are not acting biblically unless supernatural healings are taking place and occurring on an impressive scale. While I do believe in the miraculous, I am less convinced that is what this verse means, because it proves too much. If it is referring to signs and wonders, who can claim to have done anything greater than Jesus on that score? I would love to meet someone who has instantaneously healed someone born blind? I would be intrigued to talk to someone who has revived a corpse that had been rotting in the grave for four days. Can it really be the case that Jesus (the incarnate Son of God) is saying that we will be able to perform greater miracles than these? I very much doubt it.

The question we must ask is: what was the

work Jesus came to do? Surely it was to bring about believers – those who put their trust in him. This, after all, is the main thrust and purpose of the whole of John's Gospel (20:31). At one point people asked Jesus what work does God require of them, and he replied: 'The work of God is this: to believe in the one he has sent' (John 6:29). Indeed, the whole of John chapters 14-16 focus on the future work of the Holy Spirit, which is to produce believers in Jesus Christ.

Jesus' success in this realm was obviously limited during his earthly life – only a handful of people believed in him. But all that was to change at Pentecost with the giving of the Holy Spirit, so that what began as a few was to turn into the many. What was veiled and difficult to understand before Jesus' death and resurrection, was to become much clearer after those events, and especially with the sending of the Holy Spirit in power to enable people to believe. This is the greater things of which Jesus speaks. What was limited in location and people in Jesus' day, was to become unlimited and open to all after Pentecost. There is nothing more miraculous than the conversion of a rebel to Christ. This is very important.

We do not read that there is rejoicing among the angels over one cripple who is healed, but we do read of rejoicing over one sinner that repents (Luke 15:7).

There is the example of the alcoholic who was converted and gained a victory over his drink problem. As he began to put his life back together, he received more than his fair share of jibes from his friends at work over his new-found faith in Christ. One day his workmates were taunting him about miracles: 'Go on,' they said, 'you don't believe in miracles and all that turning water into wine stuff, do you?' To which he replied: 'I have never seen water turned into wine. But I have seen beer turned into furniture.'

That is what Christ can do. I know, I have seen it. This is the greater work which God is doing today.

10

Jesus meets a backslider
(John 21:15-19)

In his very challenging and helpful book, *Discipleship*, the late David Watson wrote these words:

> The vast majority of Western Christians are church-members, pew-fillers, hymn-singers, sermon-tasters, Bible-readers, even born again believers or Spirit-filled charismatics – but not true disciples of Jesus. If we were willing to learn the meaning of real discipleship and actually to become disciples, the church in the West would be transformed, and the resultant impact on society would be staggering.[1]

However, this raises the further question: how do we become disciples? How do we change into one who is willing to take up a cross and follow his Lord? We are given a wonderful insight into how this can happen in the moving encounter, recorded

---

1. *Discipleship*, David Watson, Hodder and Stoughton, 1984.

by John in his final chapter, between a discredited Peter and a risen Saviour.

The reality of Christian forgiveness

Picture the scene. In the early morning light the disciples are sitting around a camp fire on the beach, eating freshly caught fish in the presence of the risen Jesus. They can still hardly believe their eyes. Just as they are eating their last mouthful, Jesus turns to Peter and, pointing to the other disciples, asks: *'Simon son of John, do you truly love me more than these?'* (21:15).

Notice how measured and restrained Peter's reply is: *'Yes, Lord, you know that I love you.'* Whether it is more than the other disciples, he can't say, and how could he after his previous boast before the betrayal of Jesus: 'Even if the others should forsake you, Lord, I won't'?

'Feed my lambs,' replies Jesus.

A few moments later, still in full view of the disciples, Jesus turns, and looking Peter straight in the eye, asks a second time: *'Simon son of John, do you truly love me?'*

By now Peter must have felt puzzled, wondering what lay behind the question. Jesus knows everything, he has already demonstrated that. He can see directly into the human heart, so there is no point in trying to pull the wool over his eyes. *'Yes, Lord, you know I love you.'*

'In that case,' says Jesus, *'take care of my sheep'*.

There then follows a moment of silence. We can imagine Peter hoping, willing, that that would be the end of it, that someone would change the course of the conversation. But no. A third time Jesus asks Peter, *'Simon son of John, do you love me?'*

Now that hurt. For by asking this question a *third* time a nightmarish memory was dragged up from the dark recesses of Peter's subconscious, a memory so painful that it would have filled the whole of his being with bitter shame and loathing. For this same Peter, who for a third time was just about to claim his love for his Lord, had previously denied Jesus three times (John 18:15, 25-27).

In light of the knowledge of such an appalling act of selfishness and cowardice, how hollow the words 'I love you' must have sounded. But what else could Peter do? He couldn't deny the past, but neither could he deny his love for his Lord, however faint that love might be. And so he stammers with remorseful resignation: 'Lord, you know all things, including my failure. I can't hide that, but though it may sound so false in the light of what has gone before, I really do love you.'

Finally Jesus reiterates the commission: *'Feed my sheep.'*

We are now in a position to see that what Jesus

has been doing all along is getting Peter to experience the full force of his failure, so that he can embrace the full reality of the forgiveness Jesus offers.

The lesson is this: to experience real forgiveness by Christ first means experiencing real pain. Unfortunately there is a tendency today in Christian circles to have such a sentimental view of 'love' that the result is a cheap forgiveness which is no forgiveness at all. 'Oh, God will forgive me,' we say, 'After all it's his job.' Not so.

Jesus did not come up to Peter, put his arm around him and say, 'Peter, dear chap, do you love me? I know that you have been through such a terrible experience recently, but it's all over now, forget it.'

I suggest that such a form of Elastoplast counselling would have done Peter no good whatsoever. Superficially he may have felt alright for a while, relieved that his failure had not been mentioned. But Jesus is much more thorough than that. If Peter is going to *feel* the joy of forgiveness and have the assurance of forgiveness, then he must be brought to a position where he *feels* the pain of his failure.

So step by step Jesus brings Peter to that point of facing up to his sin and then (and only then) tasting the sweet forgiveness that Jesus brings. Like a master surgeon skilfully wielding the scalpel, Jesus removes layer after layer of self-pretence in order to expose the true self with all the good and the bad, in order that the bad might be dealt with. This is creative forgiveness involving a love that is not sentimental but radical, and therefore all the more lasting.

The truth is that he will do the same with us. We should not expect God to be indifferent to our failings, so that with a shrug of the shoulder we say, 'Never mind, God loves me and so he's bound to let me off.' It is because he loves us that he brings us under the searching light of his Word, to face up to our sin so that it can be dealt with. Hide it, repress it, ignore it and it will come back at some point in the future with a vengeance. But admit it, confess it, feel its shame, and then the Lord can remedy it, giving a true peace through the work of his Son on the cross.

Could it be that the reason why so many Christians today do not feel forgiven is because they have not known real repentance? They have been too afraid or too proud to be willing to undergo the heartache of facing up to the wrong done and taking personal responsibility for it. For unless we come to terms with the fact that there is something specific which needs forgiving, we shall never be motivated to seek forgiveness from God at all.

The call to Christian service

The fact that it is *real* forgiveness that is being
offered here is underscored by the call to Christian service: 'Feed my lambs', 'Care for my
sheep', 'Feed my sheep'. Here is tangible proof
that the forgiveness Christ brings is not mere
words but a restored relationship. As we say, ac-
tions speak louder than words. We all know of
folk who say, 'Sure I forgive you', but under their
breath they mutter, 'But don't think that I am going to trust you again, not after the way you have
let me down.' The way they treat us does not match
up to what they have said, and so we doubt the
sincerity of their forgiveness.

Imagine a man who has stolen money from the
till of his employer's department store. Later he is
stricken in his conscience by what he has done.
He goes to his employer, admits the crime and
hands the money back. His employer says: 'I forgive you. This time I won't call the police – but
you're sacked.' The man may well understand it
and see that he has been let off quite lightly.

But supposing instead the employer says: 'Yes,
I forgive you. I will not hide my disappointment
in you, or the hurt that I am feeling because you
betrayed my trust, but I forgive you. And to dem-
onstrate that, I am putting you in charge of the
whole of the finances of the store.' Could the man
doubt that the forgiveness is genuine? Of course

not. What is more, if the inner change has been true, then the kindness of his employer will spur him on to a far greater loyalty than he had before.

That is precisely the wonder of Jesus' forgiveness of Peter. Publicly Peter denied Jesus, and publicly Jesus reinstates Peter. What is more, Peter is given one of the greatest tasks that can be given to any human being – the pastoral care of Christian believers: 'Feed my sheep'.

Peter was to shepherd, or oversee, Christians, and the way he was to do that was modelled by Christ himself, as we see from Mark 6:34: 'When Jesus saw a large crowd he had compassion on them, because they were like sheep without a shepherd. So he began teaching them.'

In the Old Testament, the shepherds of Israel were the rulers of Israel, those who were to govern and guide God's people. Here Jesus sees people without a shepherd – lost, wandering aimlessly, and he is deeply moved. So what does he do? He teaches them the Word of God. That is how Jesus shepherds, and that is how he does it today in his church. He rules, guards and guides his sheep by his Word – the Bible. And that is the task Peter is given to do.

'Do you love me, Peter?' asks Jesus. 'Then feed my sheep.' This is the real test of love for Christ; the way one can gauge whether a person is not only soundly converted but growing in faith, is the level of their willingness and desire to minister to others – feed the sheep. Obviously this applies supremely to ministers, but at another level it applies to all those who are given the joy and privilege of teaching the Bible – whether one to one, or in a group. It applies to the Bible study leader, the Sunday school teacher, the youth worker, to any who bring the Word of God to bear so that God's people might grow in love and knowledge of him.

Sheep are strange animals. They can be slow, awkward, and unco-operative. But so can Christians. That is why they need good shepherds, not hirelings. Jesus described himself as the model shepherd in John 10 – the Good Shepherd – by way of contrast to the hireling, the rent-a-shepherd.

The hireling *appears* to care for the sheep, and while things are running smoothly he does. But when difficulty or trouble comes, he runs away leaving the sheep to fend for themselves. In other words, he is more interested in himself than in the sheep.

But not the good shepherd; he is willing to give his life for his sheep. He is ready to put up with all the toil, the hard work, the disappointments, which inevitably come in Christian work. And why? Because he loves God and he loves the sheep. When Jesus asks Peter: 'Do you love me?' and then gives him this marvellous task of ministry, it is not only Peter's willing acceptance to take it on which is a sign of true love for Christ. It is also a sign of true love for Christ to keep on going in Christian service. Christian work will be tough. Sometimes people won't want to hear what we say. At other times we may feel that the progress is pretty slow. But if we really love Christ, then we will stick with it.

Here is the advice of Richard Baxter, one of the greatest ministers the church has ever known. He is thinking of pastors, but what he says could equally apply to anyone working in the church. He writes:

The pastor is to have patience. We must bear with many abuses and injuries from those whom we are doing good. When we have studied with them and exalted them, and spent ourselves for them, then we may still need more patience with them. We can still expect that after we have looked upon them as our own children, that there may be some who will reject us with scorn, even hate and contempt. They will cast our kindness in our teeth with disdain and look upon us as enemies. They will do this simply because we have told them the truth. Yes, even the more we have loved them, the more they will hate us. All this has to be accepted and yet we still need unswerving and unwearied desire to do good on their behalf. In meekness we must still persist in instructing those who oppose their own best interests. God may yet lead them to repentance. Even when they scorn and reject our ministry, and tell us to mind our own business, yet we must still persevere in caring for them. For we are dealing with ill people who will reject their physician. Nevertheless, we must persist with their cure. He is indeed an unworthy doctor who will be driven away merely by the foul language of a patient.[2]

If you are involved in any way with feeding our Lord's dear sheep, don't tire, nor take it for granted, and certainly don't give up, for he has given you a privilege that not even the angels are given, as well as an opportunity to show how much you really do love him.

We can now see how real forgiveness was for Peter. He wasn't going to be paralysed by his past experience, shrinking into a shell of self-protection, excusing himself from the possibility of further hurt and failure by protesting: 'Who am I to feed God's sheep? I failed once I am bound to fail

---

2. *The Reformed Pastor*, Richard Baxter, Multnomah Press, 1982.

again, better play safe than sorry – get someone else to do it, Lord – maybe John.' I am sure we have all felt like that. But Peter wasn't going to succumb to that temptation. Having faced up to his failure and having received the forgiveness of Christ, he wanted to show that his love was more than words, by actively responding in Christian service.

The demands of Christian discipleship

More than that, however, Peter had to be willing to quite literally take up the cross of Christian discipleship: *'I tell you the truth, when you were younger you dressed yourself and went where you wanted; but when you are old you will stretch out your hands, and someone else will dress you and lead you where you do not want to go.' Jesus said this to indicate the kind of death by which Peter would glorify God. Then he said to him, 'Follow me'* (21:18-19).

Christian service is always costly, and Jesus warns Peter that he is to pay the ultimate price for following his Master – death. The term 'stretch out your hands' was used in the Roman world to describe crucifixion. The stretching took place when the prisoner was tied to the cross-member and forced to carry it to the place of execution.

What is truly remarkable is that Peter went on to serve Christ for thirty years, with this prediction hanging over him, before it eventually took place. Can we imagine that? Knowing that if we take up a particular line of Christian work, that at the end of it all lies a foul, excruciatingly painful death by torture. Can we envisage waking up each day for three decades wondering if this is going to be the day when we were going to have our hands and feet hammered into a piece of wood? How did Peter cope with that?

Peter, having received so much forgiveness from his Saviour, knew there was no greater task than to be serving his Saviour. It was this knowledge of what he had received that enabled him to go on in the face of such an appalling prospect. Love meant sacrifice, and sacrifice meant cost. But it was to be worth it. For as Peter writes out of personal experience in his first letter: 'Rejoice that you participate in the sufferings of Christ, so that you may be overjoyed when his glory is revealed' (1 Peter 4:13).

We, like Peter, have to get it firmly fixed in our minds that this life is not all there is. It is short and brief. In fact compared to eternity it is as noticeable as a blink of the eyes in a whole year. Therefore, whatever time we have left we are to use it in submitting to Christ in everything, showing that love for Christ in serving his sheep, and by crucifying the self so that Christ might be seen to live in us.

11

Jesus meets the world
(John 1:1-14)

It is often remarked that 'familiarity breeds contempt' and I guess that one of the pitfalls into which those who have been Christians for some time stumble is in taking some basic Christian truths for granted.

For example, when Christians say, 'I believe in Jesus Christ, born of the Virgin Mary', has it ever occurred to you what an amazing profession that is? For they are saying that God the Creator became a creature; that the manger in which this baby lay was held in being by the power of the one who lay in it. In short, Christians are claiming that God became a man in space-time history. There is no other religion on earth which makes such a claim.

In this final chapter we draw together some of the strands which have run throughout this book weaving a most amazing tapestry of the person of Jesus Christ. We do so by turning to the chapter which John places at the beginning of his Gospel, what is often called the 'prologue'. Without wishing to appear to question John's order by considering the first chapter last, it is hoped that that which may initially seem strange to twentieth-century ears may not seem so strange in the light of all the other 'close encounters' we have been considering.

The revelation

You may have seen one of those TV programmes, usually hosted by a bishop or a university don, to which well-known celebrities are invited. As they sit around a low coffee table upon which are placed the requisite glasses of water, they are asked to share their thoughts on what heaven will be like, or what God is like. Usually they begin by saying something like this: 'Well, I like to think ...'.

Has it ever crossed your mind what an irrelevance that is? What does it matter what a person *likes* to think? I might *like* to think that I have a million pounds in the bank, and I might *like* to act on that thought and go out and buy all sorts of things. But no matter what I like to think, the vital question remains: is it true? If not, then no amount of waffle about liking to think that I had a million pounds will satisfy a judge when I end up in court with a debt problem. So the issue is not: How do we like to think of God, but, what is he really like

– is he a 'he' at all? The critical question is: How can we know God?

The answer is that we need a revelation, with God pulling back the curtain and meeting with us in a way we can comprehend. If we cannot reach up to God (because he is infinite and we are finite), then God reaches down to us. And that is precisely what these few verses are all about – the greatest communication coup the universe has ever known.

In the beginning was the Word (1:1). What is the Word? It is God's self-expression. We tend to express ourselves by the use of words, so does God. But this is something more than God speaking.

First, this Word is eternal, 'In the beginning was the Word' – not the beginning of time, but before the beginning of anything. It is just another way of saying that this Word has always been in existence. What is more, the Word has personality: *The Word was with God* (1:1).

Here, in an eternal relationship, is love. That is why the Christian can claim that God is love, because in order to love you have to have someone to love. But whom did God love before the world was created? He loved the Word, this one who stood facing him (which is what the original wording suggests) and loving him in return. But can there be someone who is eternal, who is the self-expression of God, without being God himself? The answer is no – so John tells us: *The Word was God* (1:1).

Here we have the Word's deity. This phrase is one out of which the Jehovah Witnesses make a lot of capital. They say that in the original it does not have the definite article 'the', so it could read the 'word was a god', a divine being, but not God himself. But it is not quite as simple as that.

If John had wanted to say that Jesus was a divine being, there was a perfectly good Greek word he could have used, but he didn't. Also, if he had written 'the Word was the God', then it would have meant that *only* the Word existed – i.e. there would have been God the Word, but no God the Father. What John is making absolutely plain by putting it the way he does, is that while there is only one God, within the Godhead there is more than one person. The Word is God with God. Now do you see how, unless we had been told this, we would not have been able to work it out for ourselves? The necessity for revelation becomes obvious.

What else does John tell us about this 'Word'? For one thing, he tells us that he is the Creator: *Through him all things were made; without him nothing was made that has been made. In him was life, and that life was the light of men. The light shines in the darkness, but the darkness has not understood it* (1:3-5).

Whether we can understand it or not, whether it is the material world or the spiritual world, the Word is the one who not only brought it all into being, but keeps it in being. He is the source of all life, not simply biological life, but also spiritual life, and that is why he is the 'light of men'.

Both the Bible and experience confirm that we are spiritual beings, having eternity engraved on our minds – a God-awareness if you will. Even in the former Soviet Union at the height of communism, when people were being taught in the schools and universities 'There is no God', the authorities were scandalized to discover that a generation brought up on atheism were scratching prayers on the tombstones of their relatives to 'the unknown God'. We can't escape it.

We may rebel against it, but we are made for God and deep down we know it. Just as our stomachs are made for food, and when we are not fed we feel pangs of hunger (which when severe will make us eat almost anything), so we are made for something more than the material. We have a spiritual side to our nature and we will try to satisfy it in some way. Man is a religious animal. The variety of religions which exist simply bears witness to what John says: *'that light was the life of men'*; everyone is aware of God.

But when the light of God does shine in all its purity, truth and wholesomeness, we can be sure that the darkness into which it shines cannot cope with it: *'The darkness has not understood it.'* We could translate it better: 'The darkness has not mastered it.' Not only can evil not fathom God's light at work, it cannot overcome it, so evil will never ultimately win. That is a truth we really do need to hold on to when we see so much evil at work in the world – turmoil on the African continent, ethnic unrest in the Balkans, drug dealing and shootings in Manchester, the increasing pressure for euthanasia. The light will not be quenched, although there have been times in history when it has shone dimly – but the light will shine on.

So, yes, we can see something of God's character reflected in creation; yes, we can sense something of him in our hearts, but it is still all rather vague and unclear. That is, until the Word became focused in a human being: *The Word became flesh and lived for a while among us. We have seen his glory, the glory of the one and only, who came from the Father, full of grace and truth* (1:14).

This Word, the Son of God, whom John identifies in verse 17 as the carpenter from Nazareth – Jesus – became a man. We are not talking of some extra-terrestrial visitor who quickly 'beams' down to reconnoitre the earth and quickly 'beams' back again (a heresy called gnosticism). We are speaking of the one who created the glorious process of human development in the womb undergoing that process himself.

What better way for the personal God to express himself to personal beings than by becoming one of them? God's personal self-expression became a man in history. That is why his glory, his goodness, was seen by John. His goodness was transparent in what he said and the way he said it, as well as through what he did and the way he did it. He spoke as only God could speak – he forgave sins. He acted as only God could act; he raised the dead.

No-one has ever seen God, but God the One and Only [Son], who is at the Father's side, has made him known (1:18). No-one has ever seen God face to face – that is impossible, but God the only Son has made him known, and the term used there means he has narrated God to us: exegeted him.

Imagine you are at home watching TV and there appears a complicated scientific programme. By yourself it makes very little sense to you – the complex diagrams, the lengthy formulae and bewildering jargon. It looks as if it is going to be a complete waste of time and you are about to switch off when you hear the voice of the *narrator* who, in language you can understand, explains it all to you. Well, Jesus is like that narrator, for he 'narrates' God to us in his person.

If we really want to know what God is like, then let us look to Jesus who, in the plainest way possible, presents God before our very eyes. For us that means paying close attention to those who met him, or who knew those who met him; the New Testament writers.

The reaction

What was the response to the Creator coming to his creation? The red-carpet treatment maybe? Unfortunately not: *He was in the world, and though the world was made through him, the world did not recognise him. He came to that which was his own, but his own did not receive him* (1:10-11).

We may say, that is not at all surprising; who would have expected to look at a thirty-year-old carpenter made of flesh and blood and conclude that he is God? Had we been a casual observer at the time we may have seen nothing more than an interesting, and maybe even remarkable, man – but God?

Again we are coming at things from the wrong direction. We are approaching the matter with *our* expectations of what God is like and what we would do if we were God, and trying to fit the data into a preconceived mould. But we certainly wouldn't do anything like what John says happened!

That is why, therefore, we humbly need to come before the Bible and put to one side our prejudices and see what God has actually done, and be surprised (this is called the inductive approach).

This is one of the reasons why I do accept what the Bible writers say to be true: no-one could have made this up, it goes against all human ideas and expectations.

If you like, it is so remarkable it has to be true! If you were given a blank piece of paper and were told to write a story of how you think God might come in to the world, it wouldn't even remotely resemble anything like this.

But while we may give the casual observer the benefit of the doubt in not recognizing Jesus as the Son of God, what about Israel, God's own people? After all, we would have thought that they would have been at an advantage, having the Old Testament Scriptures in which God told them what he was like, and what he would do, pointing to the time when he would send his Servant, born of a virgin, to fulfil his promises. But notice that John does not say that they did not recognize him, but that they did not 'receive' him.

It would be all too easy to pride ourselves and say, 'Ah well, they should have known better, what privileges they had. But we would have received him had we been there.'

Really? Did Israel know and enjoy God's blessing for centuries? So has Britain. For a thousand
years Christianity has been the official faith of this
land. God delivered us from paganism in the
distant past, from Islam in the Middle Ages, from
a perverted Roman Catholicism in the sixteenth
century, and from Fascist and Marxist dictator-
ships in the twentieth century. He has raised up
godly men who have been burned alive so that we
could get a Bible in English. He has used men to
bring revivals and so transformed the social map
of Britain. God has spared us in so many ways.

But what do we see today?

For all the opportunities people have to come to
Christ, the churches that are on their doorstep, not
to mention the abundance of Christian literature,
for all this, we see a society which, in effect,
couldn't care less when it comes to considering
Jesus Christ. Should we be so surprised that politi-
cally, morally and spiritually we as a nation are
finding ourselves bankrupt and struggling? Of
course not. Let us not think that the reaction of the
people to Jesus' coming then was any different to
people's reaction to him today; it is not.

Why did he come?
With the coming of Jesus into the world our
deepest need was exposed once and for all. It is so
easy to look down on the other fellow and say,

'Well, at least I am not that bad.' But when we begin to measure ourselves up against this man Jesus – God's standard for living – we realize how pitiful we all are.

But that is just the starting point for those who dare look at their lives in the light of the life of Jesus and recognize they are spiritually sick. They can find healing. Those who know that left to themselves they could never find God and could never satisfy him because they don't measure up to their own standards let alone his, soon discover the most wonderful thing – they discover that they do find God in all his love and mercy in Jesus.

They begin to realize that they are not only accepted by him, forgiven, having their lives cleaned inside and out, but that they are called, for the very first time, 'God's children'.

Yet to all who received him, to those who believed in his name, he gave the right to become children of God – children born not of natural descent, nor of human decision, or a husband's will, but born of God (1:12-13).

Do you become a Christian simply by virtue of being born in Britain or baptised into the Church of England or any other denomination? No, these are children not born of 'natural descent'. Do you become a Christian because your parents or husband or wife are Christian? No, these are not children 'born of a husband's will'. Maybe you become a Christian simply by deciding to become one, by filling in a form? Again no, these are children not born of 'human decision'.

It is all very plain; there is only one way you can become a Christian and that is by a supernatural act of God in your life, being 'born of God'. Just as Mary, the mother of Jesus, couldn't decide or will for the eternal Son of God to be implanted in her womb, it was solely an act of God the Holy Spirit, humbly accepted by faith, so it is for anyone who wants to become a child of God.

After all that you have read, have you yet come to that point where you have personally received Jesus Christ? Do you see him as the Son of God, who is to be worshipped with the whole of your life? Do you see him as the one who died on the cross to save you and to take you to be with him in eternity? Do you love him? For one thing is sure, he loves you.

Melvin Tinker is Vicar of St. John's Newland in Hull. He read theology at Oxford and trained for ordination at Wycliffe Hall, before becoming a curate at Wetherby Parish Church in Yorkshire. Prior to his current position he was Anglican Chaplain to the University of Keele in Staffordshire. He has written on a wide variety of subjects relating to doctrine and ethics and was the editor of *Restoring the Vision - 'Anglicans Speak Out'* (Monarch, 1990) and *The Anglican Evangelical Crisis!* (Christian Focus Publications, 1995). He is married to Heather and they have three boys.